Fourth edition

New Headway

Upper-Intermediate Workbook with key

John and Liz Soars
Jo McCaul

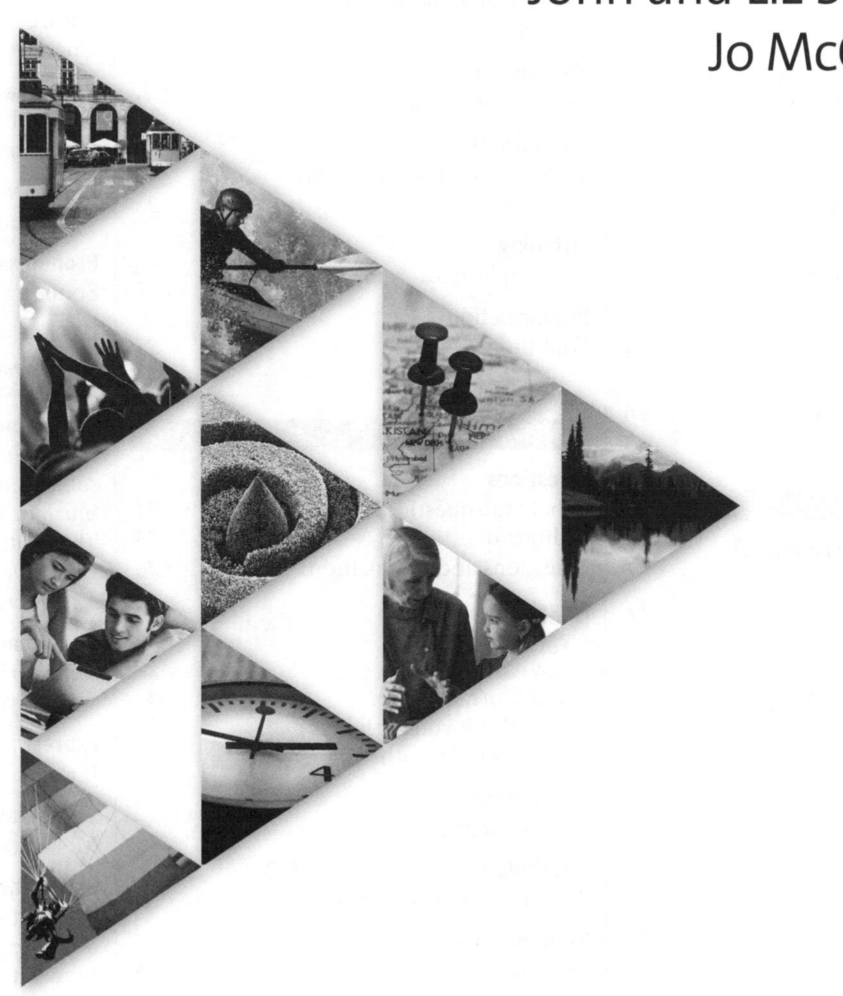

Contents

Go to **elt.oup.com/student/headway** to access the audio.

1

The tense system • *have/have got* • Compound nouns
• Phrasal verbs – literal and idiomatic • Sounds and spelling

Home and away!

The tense system

1 Identifying tenses

1 Write the correct verb form, active or passive, using the verb in the box.

walk

1 **A** How did you get here?
  B We *walked*. It didn't take long.
2 'Hello Mary? It's me. Listen, I ______ just ______ up your road – I'll be with you in five minutes!'
3 I need to sit down. We __________ for hours.

take

4 It was a hard match. At half-time, one of the footballers __________ to hospital.
5 This shirt fits me perfectly. I __________ it.
6 My dog looked guilty. He __________ some food from the kitchen table.

have

7 We need a new car. We __________ this one for ages.
8 We __________ a lovely picnic until my wife was stung by a bee.
9 Don't phone at 8.00. We __________ dinner then.

make

10 Our sandwiches ______ freshly ______ daily.
11 Have you heard about Lenny? He __________ redundant.
12 By the time I'm 40, I __________ enough money to retire.

wash

13 **A** Where are my jeans?
  B They __________ at the moment.
14 My favourite white T-shirt went pink. It __________ with my daughter's red jumper.
15 Simon was all wet because he __________ the car.

sell

16 My sister __________ her home-made cakes at the market on Saturdays.
17 If no one offers to buy the house, it __________ by auction next month.
18 I wish I'd bought that antique chair I saw. I'm sure it *will have been sold* by now.

teach

19 At the end of this term, I __________ for six years.
20 The children __________ how to make cakes when one boy dropped his bowl on the teacher's foot.

2 Complete the chart with the verb forms from exercise 1.

Active	Simple	Continuous
Present		
Past	*walked*	
Future		
Present Perfect		
Past Perfect		
Future Perfect		
Passive	**Simple**	**Continuous**
Present		
Past		
Future		
Present Perfect		
Past Perfect		
Future Perfect	*will have been sold*	

2 Check it

Correct the sentences.

1 ~~I work~~ **I'm working** hard at the moment because I have exams next week.
2 It's really cold lately, so I've bought a new winter coat.
3 Manchester United play really well at the moment. Their new player has real talent.
4 I've heard you are passing all your exams. Congratulations!
5 I was doing my homework when my friend was calling.
6 When I was a little girl, I've always spent my pocket money on sweets.
7 I went out with Paulo for two years now, and we're still crazy about each other.
8 I can't decide what to buy my brother for his birthday. Perhaps I'm going to get him a new shirt.
9 A one-day strike has called by French air traffic control for this Friday.
10 The teacher said that Megan had been working hard and was deserved to pass all her exams.

3 Using the correct tense

Read the Skype conversation between Nicola in Australia and her parents in Britain. Put the verbs into the correct tense.

SKYPING THE FOLKS

N Hello! Dad, I [1] __________ (look) at the top of your head at the moment! Reposition the camera so I can see your face.

D Sorry, I just [2] __________ (not understand) this technology. I [3] _____ only just _____ (learn) how to text! Oh my! I can't believe it. I can see you on my computer screen Nicola! I [4] __________ (call) your mum. Jackie, come here quick!

N Dad, you're so funny. I [5] __________ (do) this for ages with my friends. It's so good to see your face. I [6] __________ (not see) you for so long!

D How are the children? They look so grown up in those photos you [7] __________ (email) us.

N They're fine. Ollie [8] __________ (study) for his Year 12 Certificate. He hopes he [9] __________ (accept) at the University of Melbourne next year. Becky [10] __________ (choose) to play for her university netball team – she's so pleased. Anyway, how are you and Mum? Where is she? I want to speak to her.

D She [11] __________ (get) a bit deaf. I [12] __________ (shout) louder. Jackie, come here! It's Nicola. Anyway, where was I? We're both fine. We [13] __________ (go) on holiday last month but we just [14] __________ (stay) at a cheap bed and breakfast in Brighton to get some sea air. We [15] __________ (save) hard at the moment to come and see you at Christmas. I [16] __________ (not realize) how expensive flights are. At last! Here's your mum. Jackie, what [17] _____ you _____ (do)?

M Sorry, I [18] __________ (not hear) you. Oh my! It's our Nicola on the computer, as clear as can be. Hi, darling! I wish I could give you a big hug.

N Me too, Mum. Not long now before you and Dad [19] __________ (be) here. At least now we can see each other. Now you know what to do, we can Skype every weekend.

M Lovely, we [20] __________ (look forward to) that. Anyway, tell us how you are, darling …

Listen and check.

Passives

4 Active or passive?

1 These active sentences can sound unnatural. Rewrite them using the passive.

1 They built our house in the 17th century.

_______________________________________.

2 Someone's decorating my flat at the moment.

_______________________________________.

3 Has someone fixed the coffee machine yet?

_______________________________________?

4 We ate in restaurants while they were building the new kitchen.
While the new kitchen _______________________
_______________________________________.

5 When we went up to our hotel room, we found that someone hadn't cleaned it.

_______________________________________.

6 They won't recognize her in those dark glasses.
She _______________________________________.

2 Put the verbs in brackets into the correct tense and form, active or passive.

1 The burglars __________ (catch) as they __________ (leave) the office.

2 The postbox _____ always _____ (empty) at 12 noon.

3 Her neighbours __________ (grant) permission to build a huge extension.

4 We __________ (drive) down a quiet country lane when suddenly we __________ (overtake) by a police car.

5 When I woke up this morning, the world looked magical. It __________ (snow) all night.

6 When you __________ (arrive) in New York, you __________ (pick up) by one of our drivers and taken to the conference centre.

5 Tense review

1 Put the verbs into the correct tense, active or passive, positive or negative.

Living abroad

My name is Matt Perry and I'm 14 years old. My family [1] __________ (move) to Japan from Denver, Colorado three years ago, and we [2] __________ (live) in Tokyo for the past two years. At first it was a real culture shock and I [3] __________ (think) I'd never fit in, but now Tokyo feels just like home, and I [4] __________ (miss) it when we go back to Denver next year.

Why did we move?

My dad's an officer in the US Air Force and he [5] __________ (be/relocate) to work in other countries several times. In the past, Mum and I stayed in Denver, but we [6] __________ (not want) to be apart from my dad again, so this time we all moved. We [7] __________ (be) here for four years by the time we return home. That's the longest my dad [8] __________ (live) anywhere since he was my age.

2 Here are the answers to some questions about Matt. Complete the questions.

1 How _______________________________?
For three years.

2 Where _______________________________?
Denver, Colorado.

3 Why _______________________________?
His father was relocated there.

4 What _______________________________?
He joined a football club.

5 What ____________________ for three years?
Japanese.

6 Why _______________________________?
Because the characters are confusing.

7 What _______________________________?
TV and comics.

8 When _______________________________?
Next year.

What's it like in Japan?

I [9] ______ always ______ (think) that Japanese people were quite reserved, but they're really sociable. When we first arrived, I [10] ______ (join) a football club and I [11] ______ (make) lots of American, English, and Japanese friends. I [12] ______ (learn) the language for three years now and my Japanese friends say I'm pretty good. But I [13] ______ (not like) writing Japanese because I always [14] ______ (get) confused by the characters.

What do I miss most?

I miss the TV and my comics, though it [15] ______ (get) better all the time. Soon I [16] ______ (be able to) buy my favourite American comic here. I also miss basketball, which was my favourite sport before we came to Japan. My mum [17] ______ (miss) her garden because we [18] ______ (not live) in a house, but a fourth-floor apartment. Anyway, we [19] ______ (be) back in Denver next year and I'm sure we [20] ______ all ______ (miss) so many things about Japan.

I know I'm only 14, but I've learned an awful lot about myself from living abroad. I'm going to feel very grown up compared to the other kids when I get home.

Auxiliary verbs

6 *have*, *be*, or *do*?

Complete the sentences with the correct form of *have*, *be*, or *do*. Write **A** for an auxiliary verb and **F** for a full verb. Sometimes the auxiliary is negative.

1 [A] They **had** finished supper when we arrived.
2 [F] We **didn't have** pizza for supper last night.
3 [ ] It ______ been a lovely day. Thank you.
4 [ ] I always ______ a shower after work.
5 [ ] I ______ always had a passion for Indian food.
6 [ ] Maria overslept, so she ______ catch her train.
7 [ ] What have you ______ to your hair? You look awful!
8 [ ] What ______ your new boyfriend look like?
9 [ ] This graffiti ______ done by British artist Banksy.
10 [ ] My boiler ______ being repaired at the moment.
11 [ ] I hate ______ the washing-up. I'd like a dishwasher.
12 [ ] I ______ my homework very quickly last night.

have or *have got*?

7 Forms of *have* and *have got*

Complete the conversations with a form of *have* or *have got*. Sometimes both forms are possible.

1 **A** Rebecca, ______ you ______ a headache?
B Yes, I ______ difficulty sleeping at the moment.
A Oh dear. Why is that?
B Oh, the usual money worries. ______ you ______ an aspirin?

2 **A** ______ you ______ any pets?
B No, we ______ . ______ you?
A Oh yes. I ______ pets all my life. At the moment, I ______ a dog, two cats, and two mice.
B I'd love ______ a dog, but I'm not so sure about mice!

3 **A** Come on! We ______ to hurry. We're late!
B But I ______ my passport. I can't find it anywhere!
A You ______ it yesterday. ______ a look in your bag.
B I ______ it! You were right.

4 **A** I'm looking forward to ______ a few days' holiday. I ______ so much work for the past couple of months. I ______ a break for ages.
B You're lucky! I ______ any holiday left!

Vocabulary

8 Compound nouns

Write one word to make three compound nouns. Check the use of hyphens, one word, or two words in your dictionary.

1 ______ test / pressure / donor

2 ______ worm / shelf / cover

3 ______ fall / melon / skiing

4 ______ fingers / house / salad

5 ______ club / mare / time

6 brief / suit / book ______

7 tea / make-up / plastic ______

8 ______ bow / coat / drop

9 ______ shine / rise / set

10 ______ works / sign / map

11 ______ line / conditioning / fare

12 ______ light / break / dream

13 ______ shake / writing / bag

14 ______ cube / berg / rink

15 ______ scape / lady / slide

16 birthday / credit / business ______

17 ______ car / man / wear

18 note / address / visitors' ______

9 *house* and *home* idioms

1 Tick (✓) the correct definition for each idiom. Use your dictionary.

1 They get on like a house on fire.
 a ☐ They have a very good relationship.
 b ☐ They are always arguing.

2 Come in and make yourself at home.
 a ☐ Tidy the house.
 b ☐ Please behave in my house as if it were yours.

3 Lloyd Webber's new musical brought the house down.
 a ☐ The musical was a success.
 b ☐ The musical wasn't a success.

4 The news report really brought home to me the horrors of famine.
 a ☐ The report talked about the horrors of famine.
 b ☐ The report made me realize fully the horrors of famine.

5 These drinks are on the house.
 a ☐ These drinks are very pricey.
 b ☐ These drinks are free of charge.

6 This shaky old bridge is actually (as) safe as houses.
 a ☐ Don't worry. The bridge is very safe.
 b ☐ Be careful. The bridge isn't safe at all.

2 Complete the conversations with the idioms from exercise 1 in the correct form.

1 **A** I was so sorry to hear that your cat died.
 B Thank you. When I saw her empty bowl, it really ______________________ the fact that I'd never see her again.

2 **A** How did the meeting with Andy's parents go?
 B It was great. We all ______________________ .

3 **A** Hello! Sorry we're so late. The traffic was terrible.
 B Don't worry. Just sit down and ______________________! I'll put the kettle on.

4 **A** Did you read those excellent reviews in the local paper about the school play?
 B Yes, I did. Apparently, it ______________________!

5 **A** I'm not going up there. It looks a bit dangerous!
 B Oh, come on! It's ______________________, and the view from the top is fantastic!

6 **A** How was that new restaurant you went to?
 B Well, the food was overpriced, but the manager gave us champagne ______________________ because it was my birthday!

Phrasal verbs

10 Literal and idiomatic meanings

Phrasal verbs sometimes have a literal meaning, and sometimes an idiomatic meaning:

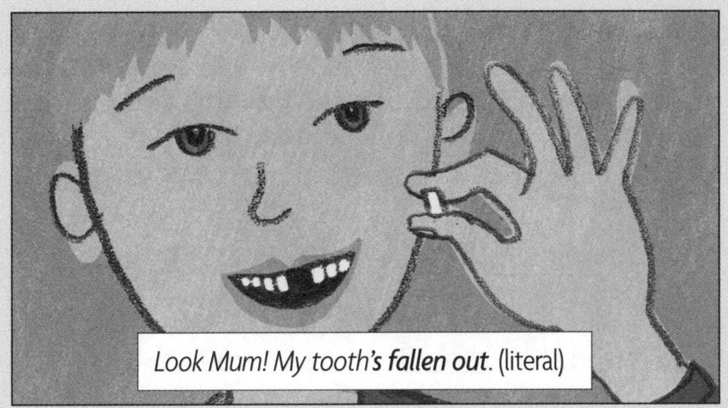

Look Mum! My tooth's ***fallen out****.* (literal)

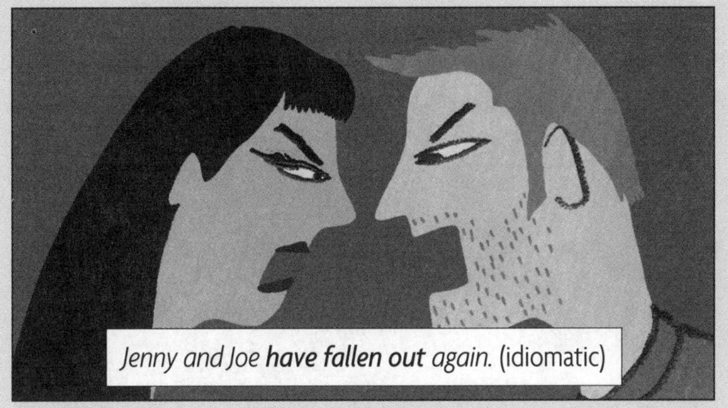

Jenny and Joe ***have fallen out*** *again.* (idiomatic)

Literal

1 Complete the sentences with a particle from the box. Some are used more than once.

away on off back out down in

1. The dentist said my tooth was bad. He had to pull it ___________ .
2. Don't run ___________ ! Come here! I want to talk to you.
3. My aunt fell ___________ the stairs and broke her leg.
4. I fell ___________ my horse!
5. When the sun went ___________ , it was really cold.
6. A button has come ___________ my shirt. Could you sew it back ___________ for me?
7. I don't feel like cooking tonight. Shall we eat ___________ instead?
8. I'm going to the library to take ___________ the books I've finished.
9. I've just hung the washing out, and it's starting to rain. Can you help me to bring it ___________ ?
10. Don't throw the box ___________ . I'm sure I can use it for something.

Literal or idiomatic?

2 Complete the pairs of sentences with the same phrasal verb from the box in the correct form. Write **L** for a literal meaning and **I** for an idiomatic one.

take off pick up sort out put up stand up hold on

1 ☐ I'm coming to London for an interview next week – can you ___________ me ___________ for the night?

☐ ___________ your hand if you know the answer.

2 ☐ I ___________ all my clothes drawers today, so now I know where everything is.

☐ We've got a problem here, but if we try hard, I'm sure we can ___________ it ___________ .

3 ☐ When I was at school, we had to ___________ when the teacher came in the room.

☐ You shouldn't let your sister tell you what to do all the time. You should ___________ for yourself more, and say what you think.

4 ☐ It's too warm to be wearing a jumper. Why don't you ___________ it ___________ ?

☐ After a slow start, my business finally started to ___________ .

5 ☐ I was never taught how to cook. I just ___________ it ___________ from my mother.

☐ Can you please ___________ the chocolate wrapper you have just dropped!

6 ☐ **A** Can I speak to Kate, please?
B ___________ . I'll just get her.

☐ When you're riding on the back of a motorbike, you have to ___________ tight.

Listening

11 Missing home

1 Listen to Nancy and Amy, two first-year university students, talking about living away from home. Tick (✓) the things they miss.

1 ☐ boyfriend
2 ☐ dad's chicken curry
3 ☐ friends from home
4 ☐ living in a house
5 ☐ being looked after by parents
6 ☐ family pet

2 Listen again. Mark the sentences true (✓) or false (✗).

1 ☐ Nancy's mum bought her a cake.
2 ☐ Nancy likes the chips in the canteen.
3 ☐ Nancy and Amy do lots of cooking.
4 ☐ Everyone else seems to be having a good time.
5 ☐ Nancy likes going out all the time.
6 ☐ The communal kitchen is very clean.
7 ☐ Amy likes being more independent.

3 Look at the tapescript on p83. Find examples of missing words in the conversation.

Pronunciation

12 Vowel sounds and spelling

1 Each of these words in phonetics has a different English vowel sound. Listen and write the words.

▶▶ **Phonetic symbols p100**

1 /frend/	_____	7 /fænz/	_____
2 /ˈɪŋglɪʃ/	_____	8 /bɒks/	_____
3 /kliːn/	_____	9 /θɔːt/	_____
4 /mʌnθ/	_____	10 /wɜːk/	_____
5 /tʊk/	_____	11 /tʃɑːt/	_____
6 /njuːz/	_____	12 /ˈwɪntə/	_____

2 Complete the chart with the words from the box. There are three words for each vowel sound.

~~letter~~	busy	water	woman
~~freak~~	dead	drew	suspicious
decide	alarm	business	drop
barrier	birth	adopt	culprit
sweeper	earth	lethal	abroad
beggar	far	orphanage	shelter
zoom	father	couple	autobiography
family	Sir	accident	shock
rough	should	goodness	suitable

/e/	/ɪ/	/iː/	/ʌ/
letter	_____	freak	_____
_____	_____	_____	_____
_____	_____	_____	_____
/ʊ/	**/uː/**	**/æ/**	**/ɒ/**
_____	_____	_____	_____
_____	_____	_____	_____
_____	_____	_____	_____
/ɔː/	**/ɜː/**	**/ɑː/**	**/ə/**
_____	_____	_____	_____
_____	_____	_____	_____
_____	_____	_____	_____

Listen and check.

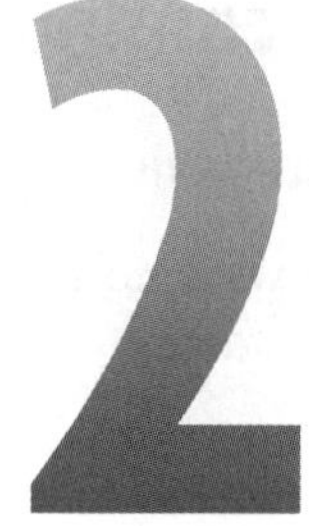

Present Perfect • Simple and continuous
• *have something done* • Travel and transport
• Prepositions of movement • Word stress

Been there, got the T-shirt!

Simple or continuous verb forms?

1 Present Perfect Simple or Continuous?

Match the lines to make sentences.

	A	B
1	a He's written b He's been writing	three magazine articles so far. a travel blog since he left home.
2	a They've missed b They've been missing	you lots, so come home soon. the bus again.
3	a Paula's been leaving b Paula's left	work early to run some errands. work early all this week.
4	a I've lost b I've been losing	weight recently. my car keys.
5	a She's been talking b She's talked	on the phone for ages. about this subject before.
6	a The cat's been going b The cat's gone	next door to have its dinner. upstairs.
7	a He's had b He's been having	a heart attack. second thoughts about the job.
8	a I've been saving up b I've saved up	to buy a brand new 52-inch TV. about £500.
9	a I've been swimming, b I've swum	20 lengths today. which is why my hair is wet.
10	a I've been finding b I've found	my cheque book at last. it hard to concentrate recently.

2 Turning mountains of rubbish into gold.

Read the article and circle the correct verb form.

Turning mountains of rubbish into gold

Mount Everest is the highest mountain in the world, but unfortunately it is one of the messiest, too. Nearly 4,000 people [1] *have climbed / have been climbing* the 29,035-foot Mount Everest since the New Zealander Sir Edmund Hillary and Sherpa Tenzing first [2] *scaled / were scaling* its heights in 1953. But, unlike Hillary and Tenzing, these adventure tourists [3] *have dumped / have been dumping* tonnes of used equipment on Everest's slopes. Buried under snow in the winter, this junk is revealed in summer when the snow [4] *melts / is melting.*

However, now 15 Nepalese artists [5] *turn / are turning* the junk into art. They [6] *have worked / have been working* for a month to transform eight tonnes of Everest rubbish into 75 sculptures, which [7] *are now shown / are now being shown* at a hotel in the Nepalese capital, Kathmandu.

The rubbish used in the artworks [8] *was collected / was being collected* by Sherpa climbers. It [9] *includes / is including* old rope, tent poles, oxygen cylinders, drink cans, and even the remains of a helicopter. Kripa Rana Shahi, the project organizer, [10] *looked / was looking* for a way to spread awareness about keeping Everest clean when she [11] *had / was having* the ingenious idea of recycling the rubbish as works of art. She believes that Everest is Nepal's 'crown jewel'.

The sculptures [12] *range / are ranging* in price from $15 to $2,300. A percentage of the money [13] *will have gone / will be going* to the artist and the rest to the Everest Summiteers Association (ESA).

'Garbage on Everest is shameful.' says ESA chief, Wangchu Sherpa. 'We [14] *try / are trying* to turn it into gold here.'

Tortoise created out of discarded oxygen cylinder.

Mount Everest's rubbish turned into an art exhibition.

3 Present Perfect and Past Simple

Look at the Wallenda family's history. Complete the questions and answers.

The Flying Wallendas
Seven generations of performers

1700s	The Wallenda family began their career as circus performers.
Late 1800s	The Wallendas were known throughout Europe as the masters of the flying trapeze.
1920	Karl Wallenda first walked the tightrope without a net.
1928	All the Wallendas performed at Madison Square Garden where they walked the tightrope without a net after it was lost in shipping.
1944	The whole family fell off the tightrope in Ohio and survived. Thereafter, they became known as The Flying Wallendas.
1962	Two family members died when a seven-person pyramid went tragically wrong.
1963	Karl's sister-in-law, Rietta, fell to her death aged 43.
1978	Karl died after falling from a tightrope strung between two hotels in Puerto Rico. He was 73.
1979	Nik Wallenda was born in Sarasota, Florida.
1985	Nik decided he would walk a tightrope over the Niagara Falls one day – he was only six years old!
2001	The Flying Wallendas set a Guinness World Record with the first ever eight-person pyramid.
2012	Nik Wallenda fulfilled his childhood dream by walking a tightrope across the Niagara Falls.
2013	Nik Wallenda completed a quarter-mile-long tightrope walk, 1,500 feet over the Grand Canyon.

1 How long have the Wallenda family been performing?
Since ______________________________ .

2 What ______ the Wallendas ______ as in the late 1800s?
The masters of the flying trapeze.

3 Why __________ the Wallendas ________________________
without a net?
Because they lost it in shipping.

4 What __________________________ to the whole family in Ohio?
They ____
____ .

5 How long ___________ they ___________ The Flying Wallendas?
___________ 1944.

6 ___________ Rietta when she ___________ to her death?
Only 43.

7 Where and when _______________ Nik ___________________ ?
In Sarasota ______________________________ .

Simple or continuous review

4 Niagara daredevil

1 Read the news article and circle the correct verb form.

Friday June 15

NIAGARA DAREDEVIL

Tomorrow will be a historic day if Nik Wallenda [1] *becomes / is becoming* the first person in more than a century to cross the Niagara Falls from the US to Canada on a tightrope.

For nearly 30 years, Wallenda [2] *has tried / has been trying* to persuade the Niagara Parks Commission in Canada to let him walk across the Falls. At last, he [3] *has granted / has been granted* permission for the stunt to take place.

Daredevil Nik is a member of The Flying Wallendas, a family of circus performers spanning seven generations, who already [4] *holds / is holding* six Guinness World Records. He [5] *started / was starting* tightrope walking at the age of two and now has over 30 years' experience.

To prepare for the event, a team of firefighters [6] *were spraying / have been spraying* gallons of water at high pressure to replicate the power of spray from the Falls. Also, he [7] *has blasted / has been blasted* by a wind machine with gusts of up to 44 miles per hour. As Nik says, [8] '*We play / We're playing* with Mother Nature and Mother Nature has a mind of her own.'

Nik [9] *traverses / will be traversing* a 1,500-foot tightrope, which [10] *will be suspending / will be suspended* 200 feet above the roaring Falls. He says he loves the sensation of peace and calm that he [11] *feels / is feeling* in the plumes of mist from the surging water.

Unbelievably, Nik [12] *didn't want / wasn't wanting* to wear a safety harness, but ABC TV, who [13] *broadcast / are broadcasting* the event, would not risk the possibility of a man falling to his death [14] *showing / being shown* on live TV.

2 Complete the sentences. Use each verb twice, once in a simple and once in a continuous tense, active or passive.

1 rain
It __was raining__ quite heavily when Nik Wallenda crossed the Niagara Falls on his tightrope.
It __rained__ for days and our road was flooded.

2 perform
Cirque du Soleil ____________ at the Royal Albert Hall since November.
David ____________ so well in his school play that he got a standing ovation.

3 have
I ____________ dinner with friends tonight.
They ____________ three children, two boys and a girl.

4 think
You look worried. What ____________ about?
I ____________ it's time you had a haircut.

5 bang
I couldn't sleep because the garden gate ____________ in the wind all night!
Ouch! I ____________ just ____________ my head on the cupboard door.

6 read
I ____________ this book since the summer and I still haven't finished it!
I was thrilled when I ____________ your email. What wonderful news!

7 fight
I ____________ long and hard for my pay rise.
Where did you get that black eye from? ____________ with your brother again?

8 expect
Could you get off the phone? I ____________ a call.
I ____________ you are studying hard for your exams at the moment.

9 decorate
Helen's house ____________ at the moment so she's staying with a friend.
Their house ____________ in a minimalist style.

10 lose
I think I must ____________ my mind. I can't even remember what we did last weekend.
Kate is going on her honeymoon next week and she ____________ her passport!

Passive

5 Present Perfect passive

1 Rewrite the sentences using the passive and omitting the subject.

1 The bin men have already collected the rubbish.
The rubbish *has already been collected.*

2 Have the workmen repaired the street lights yet?
______________________________?

3 The government has just passed some new anti-drug laws.
Some new anti-drug laws ______________________.

4 The local council hasn't built any new homes for 20 years.
No ______________________.

5 Nobody has watered the plants.
The plants ______________________.

2 Rewrite the headlines using the Present Perfect passive.

1 **Rat Alert at Buckingham Palace**
Rats have been found at Buckingham Palace.

2 **Banker Bonuses Slashed**
______________________.

3 **Dramatic Rescue of Fishermen in Pacific**
______________________.

4 **Monsoon Kills over 400 in Pakistan**
______________________.

5 **Theft of Dalí Painting in New York**
______________________.

6 **Ancient Pyramids Discovered in Sudan**
______________________.

7 **Missing Teenager Alive**
______________________.

8 **Council Shock – 464 Jobs Axed!**
______________________.

6 *have something done*

1 Look at the difference in meaning between these sentences:
I've repaired my bicycle. = I repaired it myself.
My bicycle has been repaired. = Someone repaired it. (The action is important, not who did it.)
I've had my bicycle repaired. = I arranged/paid for someone to repair it for me. (*have* + object + past participle)

2 *Have something done* is used to talk about services that you ask someone else to do.
I'm going to ***have my hair cut.***

1 Rewrite the sentences using *have something done*.

1 John's kitchen is being decorated.
He's having his kitchen decorated.

2 My sister wants someone to pierce her ears.
She wants to ______________________.

3 My eyes are going to be tested.
I'm going to ______________________.

4 Mr and Mrs Turner's car has been serviced.
They ______________________.

5 Our television hasn't been repaired yet.
We haven't ______________________.

2 It's Melanie and Ken's wedding day. Look at the notes and write sentences about what they *have had / are having done*.

They've had the invitations printed.

She ...

He ...

Melanie & Ken
Recently – the invitations printed
– wedding dress made
– the cake decorated
Yesterday – champagne delivered
– hair cut
Today – hair styled
– flowers delivered
Next week – photos developed
– wedding dress and suit dry-cleaned

Listening

7 Off the beaten track

1 Listen to the radio programme. What do the three people do? Where did they visit?

Kay Morris

Vicky Smith

Gary Braithwaite

a ____________ c ____________ e ____________

b ____________ d ____________ f ____________

2 Listen again. Write **KM**, **VS** or **GB**. Who talks about … ?

1 an uninteresting hotel
2 a love of old western films
3 catching food to eat
4 the warm response they received from the local people
5 a sheltered childhood
6 a room with a beautiful view

3 Are the following statements true (✓) or false (✗)?

1 ☐ *Off the Beaten Track* is a radio programme that looks at different places to visit on holiday.
2 ☐ Kay has 13 years' experience in the travel business.
3 ☐ Vicky would prefer to stay in a hotel when she goes travelling from now on.
4 ☐ The Austrian B & B was much cheaper than the hotel.
5 ☐ When Gary first landed in America, he found it didn't live up to his childhood expectations.
6 ☐ The Navajo Nation feels like its part of the USA.

Vocabulary

4 The words below are all used in the listening. What collocations can you make by combining an adjective in **A** with a noun in **B**.

A	B
stunning	fire
friendly	terrace
romantic	welcome
enchanting	tourist
adventurous	views
sunlit	haunt
crackling	destination
interesting	places
enthusiastic	hotel
five-star	atmosphere
perfect	alternatives

Vocabulary

8 Travel and transport words

1 Tick the verbs which go with each form of transport.

	car	bus	bike	train	plane	ship/ ferry
get into/out of						
get on/off						
take off						
land						
ride						
drive						
catch						
miss						
board						
park						

2 Complete the table below with the nouns in the box. Some can go into more than one column.

runway	platform	seat belt
helmet	harbour	carriage
traffic lights	life jacket	service station
season ticket	trolley	tyres
track	horn	port
one-way street	check-in desk	traffic jam
baggage rack	timetable	hand luggage
Customs	deck	traffic warden
cabin	aisle/window seat	cycle lane
security check	ticket inspector	overhead locker

car	bus	bike

train	plane	ship/ferry

Prepositions

9 Prepositions of movement

Complete the text with prepositions from the box. Use each preposition at least once.

across	against	on	onto
along	in	off	into
up	out of	over	through
past	to	towards	at

Joe's journey across town

Joe's plane landed on time [1] ______ Heathrow airport. He had exactly one hour to get [2] ______ the airport and [3] ______ the centre of London to catch his train [4] ______ Manchester. He hurried [5] ______ customs and passport control, and then raced [6] ______ the taxi sign at the exit.

Unfortunately, at that moment, the strap on his rucksack broke and it fell [7] ______ his back and [8] ______ the ground. Dirty socks, shirts, and underpants spilled all [9] ______ the airport floor. Joe was so embarrassed! He stuffed everything back [10] ______ his rucksack and, pushing his way [11] ______ the crowds of people, finally made it [12] ______ the taxi rank. He jumped [13] ______ the nearest taxi, shouting 'Euston Station, quickly, please!' The taxi set off at such speed that Joe was thrown forward, hitting his face [14] ______ the glass partition. The taxi sped on and finally arrived [15] ______ the city centre, and inevitably, the middle of a traffic jam! It would be quicker to walk. Joe paid the driver, leapt [16] ______ the taxi and ran [17] ______ the pavement, [18] ______ all the brightly-lit shop windows. At last he could see the station opposite, but it was difficult to get [19] ______ the road because of all the traffic. He reached the station just as his train was leaving. He jumped [20] ______ the barrier, raced [21] ______ the platform, and leapt [22] ______ the train with seconds to spare. He sighed with relief – he would be home in time for Christmas.

Pronunciation

10 Word stress

1 Here are pairs of words in phonetic script. Look at the stress marks. Transcribe them.

▶▶ **Phonetic symbols p100**

1 /ɪk'splɔːrə/ /eksplə'reɪʃn/

2 /'pɒlətɪks/ /ˌpɒlə'tɪʃn/

3 /'fəʊtəgrɑːf/ /fə'tɒgrəfə/

4 /'lʌkʃəri/ /lʌg'ʒʊəriəs/

5 /prɒ'djuːs/ /prə'dʌkʃn/

6 /dʒə'pæn/ /dʒæpə'niːz/

🎧 Listen and practise saying them.

2 What is the stress pattern of the words in exercise 1? Write them in the chart.

•●	•●•	●••
	explorer	
••●	**••●•**	**•●••**
	exploration	

3 Write the words in the box in the chart above.

instructor	destination	illegal
adrenaline	community	reject (v)
success	backpacker	Bangladesh
paradise	infinite	packaging
scientists	Philippines	charity
disappointment	European	pollute
spectacular	afternoon	complain
memorial	Cambodia	emergency
authentic		

🎧 Listen and practise saying them.

Narrative tenses • Time expressions
• Film, theatre, books • Phrasal verbs – type 1 • Diphthongs

News and views

Narrative tenses

1 Which narrative tense?

Complete the article with the verbs in the box. Use each verb once only.

Past Simple		Past Continuous	Past Perfect Simple	Past Perfect Continuous
saved	made	was drowning	had been	had been bodyboarding
hovered	was airlifted	was struggling	had arrived	
came through	was lowered	~~was piloting~~	had seen	
swept	were		had managed	
swam				

Prince William saves drowning girl

A heroic rescue

It has emerged that Prince William [1] was piloting the Royal Air Force Sea King helicopter that [2] __________ a teenage girl from drowning off the coast of Wales. He [3] __________ on duty for only 15 minutes when a call [4] __________ that a young girl [5] __________ in the sea. In less than a minute, the Prince and his crew [6] __________ at the scene.

Girls in distress!

Thirteen-year-old Tamara West [7] __________ when a rip tide [8] __________ her out to sea. From the beach, Tamara's older sister, Sharon, [9] __________ what had happened and [10] __________ out to save her. However, in the meantime, a surfer [11] __________ to rescue Tamara, and it was now poor Sharon who [12] __________ against the strong current and the waves.

Calm and controlled

Prince William calmly [13] __________ overhead in the Sea King whilst the paramedic, Master Aircrew Harry Harrison, [14] __________ to rescue the exhausted girl from the sea. The teenager [15] __________ to hospital where she [16] __________ a full recovery.

The Prince's superior officers [17] __________ full of praise for his handling of the sea rescue.

2 Irregular verbs

1 Complete the sentences with the irregular verb in either the Past Simple or the Past Perfect.

stick ☐

1 Becky __________ her tongue out at the teacher.

2 Someone __________ the exam results on the noticeboard earlier that morning.

fall ☐

3 Harry __________ in love with a Greek girl while he was working in Athens.

4 He __________ in love before, but this was different. He wanted to marry her.

cost ☐

5 It __________ an awful lot to have our car fixed.

6 Ted told me his new car __________ a fortune.

fly ☐

7 When I went to Australia, I was nervous because I __________ (never) before.

8 The plane took off and __________ into the clouds.

catch ☐

9 Suzy wondered how she __________ a cold in the middle of her summer holiday.

10 She __________ a taxi outside the restaurant, and went back to her hotel.

be ☐

11 Talks __________ held in New York last week to discuss global warming.

12 When the politicians left the talks, no decisions __________ reached.

2 Tick (✓) the verbs in exercise 1 which have the same form for the Past Simple and the past participle.

3 Past Simple or Past Continuous?

Circle the correct tense.

1 I *lived / was living* in Eastbourne when I *met / was meeting* my husband.

2 Our team *played / was playing* really well. We *won / were winning* at half time, but in the end we *lost / were losing* 3–2.

3 I *didn't think / wasn't thinking* of having a birthday party, but now I'm glad I *had / was having* one.

4 I'm so tired. The baby next door *was coughing / coughed* all night long and we *weren't getting / didn't get* any sleep.

5 It *was snowing / snowed* when I *got up / was getting up* this morning. The children next door *made / were making* a snowman, so I quickly *put / was putting* on some warm clothes and *raced / was racing* outside to help them.

6 James *was playing / played* happily when his big brother *hit / was hitting* him on the head and *made / was making* him cry.

7 A weird thing *happened / was happening* to me yesterday. I *was walking / walk* home when I *noticed / was noticing* a light hovering above me. I *wanted / was wanting* to get a photo, but it suddenly *vanished / was vanishing* into thin air.

8 Roger *sunbathed / was sunbathing* by the hotel pool when he *heard / was hearing* a strange sound. An enormous insect *appeared / was appearing* and *landed / was landing* on his leg.

4 Time expressions

1 Match the lines and time expressions. Use each expression once only.

1 [d] I've been working in the same bank	a ten years ago.
2 [ ] I started this job	b by the time I was 40.
3 [ ] I didn't want to get married	c until I was 30.
4 [ ] I had had two children	d for years.
5 [ ] I'd been writing poetry for years	e since six o'clock.
6 [ ] I didn't stay in that job	f until I arrived.
7 [ ] I've been waiting here	g when he finally arrived.
8 [ ] They didn't order the meal	h for long.
9 [ ] The train pulled out of the station	i a minute ago.
10 [ ] I'd been waiting over an hour	j until it was too late.
11 [ ] I haven't been feeling well	k until late.
12 [ ] They got on the plane	l lately.
13 [ ] I'd never seen him	m at the last minute.
14 [ ] I was watching TV	n before.
15 [ ] He didn't hear the attacker	o before being published.

2 Complete the sentences, using past tenses only and the prompts in brackets.

1 Two years ago, while I ______________________________ .
(work / Paris / grandfather / die)

2 As soon as I ______________________________ .
(get / home / switch on the TV)

3 First I ______________________________ .
(shower / then / get dressed)

4 Since I was a child, I ______________________________ .
(always / want / visit / Australia / finally / go / last year)

5 As he ______________________________ .
(post / letter / realize / not put on / stamp)

6 By the time he'd ______________________________
______________ . (finish / speak / most / audience / fall asleep)

7 Once I'd ______________________________ .
(tell him / truth / feel better)

8 Until I ______________________________ .
(find a flat / I / stay with friends / months)

Past passives

5 Active to passive

In these sentences the subject is either not important or too obvious to be necessary. Put each sentence into the passive.

1 Someone stole my bike last night.
My bike was stolen last night.

2 Archaeologists discovered a Roman temple underneath the new housing estate.
A Roman temple ______________________________
______________________________ .

3 The sports officials held the races indoors because it was raining.
The races ______________________________
______________________________ .

4 Someone had booked the swimming pool for a children's party on Saturday afternoon.
The swimming pool ______________________________
______________________________ .

5 The plumber was repairing the dishwasher, so I couldn't leave the house.
The dishwasher ______________________________
______________________________ .

6 When we returned to our hotel room, the chambermaid still hadn't cleaned it.
Our hotel room ______________________________
______________________________ .

7 The chef hadn't cooked the fish for long enough.
The fish ______________________________
______________________________ .

8 Workmen were putting up new traffic lights at the crossroads.
New traffic lights ______________________________
______________________________ .

Revision of active and passive

6 Film review

Read the review and complete it with a verb in the correct form.

MONSTERS UNIVERSITY

release	combine	show	adore	see

When I first [1] __________ *Monsters, Inc.*, I loved it. Who didn't? In 2001, when the film [2] __________ first __________ in cinemas, monsters Mike and Sulley [3] __________ by millions. Now, over a decade later, Pixar [4] __________ the prequel *Monsters University*. This is a movie that [5] __________ the humour from the first film with the latest animated technology to create one of Pixar's most exciting films to date!

loathe	study	become	overcome	tell	work	take

In *Monsters University*, we [6] __________ back in time to Mike and Sulley's student days before they [7] __________ for *Monsters, Inc.* They are 18 years old, and they [8] __________ at the Monstropolis University of Fear. We see how the two characters [9] __________ each other when they first meet, and this mutual hatred provides a great deal of humour. *Monsters University* [10] __________ the story of how Mike and Sulley [11] __________ their differences and [12] __________ the best of friends.

make	direct	compose	achieve	find	come

Dan Scanlon [13] __________ the film, Kori Rae produced it, and Randy Newman [14] __________ the music score. This is the first prequel that Pixar [15] __________ ever __________. It was always going to be a challenge to recreate the magic of *Monsters, Inc.*, yet Pixar [16] __________ this with confidence and success. Technology [17] __________ a long way since 2001, and the computer animation is scarily realistic! The script is genius, and both parents and children [18] __________ it hilarious – a real family blockbuster.

Vocabulary

7 Film, theatre, books

Are the words connected with film (**F**), theatre (**T**), or books (**B**)? Some are connected with more than one.

act <u>F</u> <u>T</u>	director	e-reader	prequel/sequel	fairy tale	performance
plot	backstage	character	documentary	programme	thriller
storyline	trailer	musical	blockbuster	whodunnit	playwright
chapter	script	starring role	animation	science fiction	autobiography
stalls	rehearsal	novelist	screen	hardback	full house
critic	review	matinee	interval	dressing-room	paperback

Phrasal verbs

8 Type 1 – phrasal verbs with no object

There are four types of phrasal verb.

Type 1 phrasal verbs consist of a verb + adverb. There is no object.

They can be both literal and idiomatic.

She stood up and walked out. (literal)

The bomb went off. (idiomatic)

▶▶ Type 2 and type 3 p36 ▶▶ Type 4 p48

1 Match the phrasal verbs with their definitions.

1 find out	a ☐ have a more stable life
2 break up	b ☐ wait a minute
3 hold on	c ☐ be quiet
4 speak up	d 1 discover
5 set off	e ☐ be happier
6 stay in	f ☐ arrive
7 settle down	g ☐ talk louder
8 turn up	h ☐ not go out, stay at home
9 cheer up	i ☐ end a relationship
10 shut up	j ☐ begin a journey

2 Complete the sentences with the phrasal verbs from exercise 1 in the correct form.

1 Peter hasn't arrived yet – I hope he __________ soon.

2 We have a long journey tomorrow. What time are we __________?

3 Why are you so miserable? __________!

4 I don't feel like going out tonight. Let's __________ and order a pizza?

5 Larry was a bit wild at university, but then he got a job, found a lovely wife, __________ and had kids.

6 After three years of going out together, Josh and Lil eventually __________ because Josh didn't want to get married.

7 Can I copy your homework? The teacher will never __________.

8 __________! I'm trying to watch a programme and you're all talking.

9 __________! We can't hear you at the back!

10 **A** What's Bill's phone number?

B __________! I'll just look it up.

Listening

9 It's complicated!

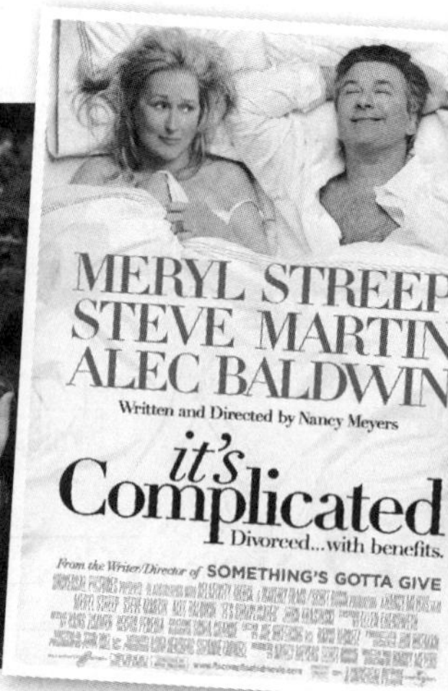

1 🎧 Listen to a conversation between two friends, Julie and Amy. (Circle) the correct answer.

1 Last Sunday, Amy *had a relaxing afternoon* / *watched a film on TV*.

2 She wants to talk to Julie about *the film she watched* / *an article she's read*.

3 In the film, Meryl Streep is the ex-wife of *Steve Martin* / *Alec Baldwin*.

4 In the film, the husband yearns for *his ex-wife* / *a new, young wife*.

5 The article and the film have *the same* / *a different* message about divorce.

6 Linda and Graham had *an acrimonious* / *a civilized* divorce.

7 They are now *dating* / *living together* again.

2 🎧 Match lines in **A** and **B** for giving and responding to news.

A
1 I think it was called 'It's complicated'.
2 It reminded me of Linda and Graham.
3 Divorced couples can become friends.
4 They've started dating again.
5 You have to work hard at relationships.
6 I hope it works out for them.

B
a ☐ They haven't! That's amazing.
b ☐ Yes, that was it.
c ☐ Did it? Why was that?
d ☐ Yes, me too.
e ☐ Actually, I can believe that.
f ☐ That's very true.

Pronunciation

10 Diphthongs

Diphthongs are two vowel sounds which run together.

hear /hɪə/ = /ɪ/ + /ə/ diphthong /ɪə/ **hair** /heə/ = /e/ + /ə/ diphthong /eə/

▶▶ Phonetic symbols p100

1 🎧 Listen and (circle) the correct transcription of each word. What is the other word? Read both aloud.

1 **pay**	/peɪ/	/peə/	3 **phone**	/fəʊn/	/faɪn/	5 **dear**	/dɪə/	/deə/	7 tour	/tʊə/	/təʊ/
2 **write**	/raɪt /	/rəʊt/	4 **round**	/reɪnd/	/raʊnd/	6 **boy**	/bəʊ/	/bɔɪ/	8 fair	/fɪə/	/feə/

2 Read the poem aloud. Write the number next to the correct sound.

Sounds and letters don't agree

When the English tongue we speak,			
Why does [1] *break* not rhyme with [2] *weak?*	2 /iː/	1 /eɪ/	
Won't you tell me why it's true			
We say [3] *sew*, but also [4] *few?*	☐ /uː/	☐ /əʊ/	
And the maker of a verse			
Cannot rhyme his [5] *horse* with [6] *worse?*	☐ /ɔː/	☐ /ɜː/	
[7] *Beard* is not the same as [8] *heard.*	☐ /ɜː/	☐ /ɪə/	
[9] *Cord* is different from [10] *word,*	☐ /ɜː/	☐ /ɔː/	
[11] *Cow* is cow, but [12] *low* is low,	☐ /aʊ/	☐ /əʊ/	
[13] *Shoe* is never rhymed with [14] *foe.*	☐ /uː/	☐ /əʊ/	
Think of [15] *hose* and [16] *dose* and [17] *lose,*	☐ /uːz/	☐ /əʊz/	☐ /əʊs/
And think of [18] *loose* and yet of [19] *choose,*	☐ /uːz/	☐ /uːs/	
Think of [20] *comb* and [21] *tomb* and [22] *bomb*	☐ /ɒm/	☐ /uːm/	☐ /əʊm/
[23] *Doll* and [24] *roll*	☐ /ɒl/	☐ /əʊl/	
and [25] *home* and [26] *some.*	☐ /ʌm/	☐ /əʊm/	
And since [27] *pay* is rhymed with [28] *say*	☐ /eɪ/	☐ /eɪ/	
Why not [29] *paid* with [30] *said,* I pray?	☐ /eɪ/	☐ /e/	
Think of [31] *blood* and [32] *food* and [33] *good;*	☐ /ʊ/	☐ /uː/	☐ /ʌ/
[34] *Mould* is not pronounced like [35] *could.*	☐ /ʊd/	☐ /əʊld/	
Why is it [36] *done,* but [37] *gone* and [38] *lone?*	☐ /əʊ/	☐ /ʌ/	☐ /ɒ/
Is there any reason known?			
To sum up, it seems to me			
That sounds and letters don't agree.			

tomb

comb

bomb

🎧 Listen and check.

Questions • Negatives • Antonyms and synonyms • Verb + preposition • Intonation in question tags

The naked truth

Questions

1 What's the question?

Read the text about Frank Abagnale and write questions for the answers.

1 Why is Frank Abagnale one of the world's most famous impersonators?
Because he assumed at least eight identities, including a pilot and a doctor.

2 ______________ was he a con man for?
Five years.

3 ______________?
Stephen Spielberg.

4 ______________ split up?
16.

5 ______________?
Bank fraud.

6 ______________ airline ______________ con?
Pan Am.

7 ______________ a paediatrician?
At a hospital in Georgia.

8 ______________?
Because he nearly caused a baby to die!

9 ______________?
Sociology.

10 ______________?
In France.

11 ______________?
Leonardo DiCaprio.

12 ______________?
He works for the FBI.

The TRUE story of a REAL fake

Frank Abagnale is one of the world's most famous impersonators. During his life, he has assumed at least eight separate identities, including an airline pilot, a lawyer, a professor, and a doctor. He was also a brilliant conman who forged $2.5 million worth of cheques across 26 countries over the course of five years. Such was his fame that his adventures have been made into a Stephen Spielberg film and a Broadway musical, both called *Catch Me If You Can.*

Amazingly, Frank's career as a conman began when he was just 16. Upset at the divorce of his parents, he ran away to New York and, being tall, handsome, and already going grey, he pretended to be 26 and got a job. His first major con was bank fraud. He created a new identity and set up numerous bank accounts. He printed flawless fake cheques and managed to cash them at the banks.

However, Frank is most famous for impersonating an airline pilot. He conned Pan Am into giving him a pilot's uniform, and he faked an ID card. He was still only a teenager when he flew over 1,000,000 miles and visited 26 countries enjoying the glamorous lifestyle of an international pilot at Pan Am's expense!

Frank also had the nerve to impersonate a paediatrician in a Georgia hospital and nearly caused a baby to die through oxygen deprivation. Having the sense to realize he was putting lives at risk, he changed course and became a university professor. He taught sociology and apparently his classes were very popular. By now, the police were on his trail, but he always managed to cover his tracks until eventually he was arrested in France and imprisoned for five years.

It is easy to understand how his amazing impersonations and adventures lent themselves to both a movie, starring Leonardo DiCaprio as Frank, and a highly successful Broadway musical.

Today, the majority of Frank's work is for the FBI, preventing fraud rather than committing it! He believes that fraud is too easy. 'Nowadays,' he says, 'technology breeds crime' and 'prevention is the only feasible course of action'.

2 Indirect questions

1 Rewrite these questions using indirect forms.

1 How many identities did he have altogether?
I'm not sure exactly *how many identities he had.*

2 How did he learn to forge cheques?
I'd like to know ______________________.

3 Why did his parents divorce?
I've no idea ______________________.

4 Who decided to make a musical?
I wonder ______________________.

5 Which countries did he visit?
I don't know ______________________.

6 How did he have the nerve to impersonate a doctor?
I can't imagine ______________________.

7 Why did the police take so long to catch him?
Do you know ______________________?

8 How did he get the job with the FBI?
I wish I knew ______________________.

2 Write indirect questions about Frank Abagnale for these answers.

1 Have you any idea ______________________?
He made millions of dollars.

2 Can you tell me ______________________?
Catch Me If You Can.

3 I wonder ______________________.
He flew for Pan Am.

4 Do you know ______________________?
Leonardo DiCaprio and Tom Hanks starred in it.

5 Why do you think he ______________________?
Because he knows better than anyone how to prevent fraud.

3 Questions and prepositions

1 Complete the questions with the prepositions in the box.

in of by with to from at about ~~for~~ on

1. What is your home town famous *for* ?
2. Who was that book written ___________ ?
3. Who does this dictionary belong ___________ ?
4. What are you looking ___________ ?
5. What did you spend all your money ___________ ?
6. What sort of books are you interested ___________ ?
7. What are you talking ___________ ?
8. What are you so afraid ___________ ?
9. Who are you angry ___________ ? James or me?
10. **A** I got these flowers in the post today!
    B Ooh, they're beautiful! Who are they ___________ ?

2 Write a short question with a preposition in reply to these sentences.

1. **A** I went to the cinema last night.
   B *Who with?*
2. **A** I'm very cross with you.
   B ___________________________________ ?
3. **A** We're going away for the weekend.
   B ___________________________________ ?
4. **A** I'm very worried.
   B ___________________________________ ?
5. **A** I'm going to Australia.
   B ___________? Two weeks? A month?
6. **A** I bought a present today.
   B ___________________________________ ?
7. **A** Have you heard? Jane has got engaged.
   B ___________________________________ ?
8. **A** Can you cut this article out for me?
   B ___________ ? I haven't got any scissors.

Negatives

4 Negative auxiliaries

Complete the sentences with the negative auxiliaries below.

isn't weren't hadn't won't aren't hasn't 'm not don't doesn't haven't didn't wasn't

1. My boss speaks fluent French, but I ___________ .
2. We wanted to leave the party, but Fred ___________ .
3. I've been to America, but my parents ___________ .
4. I thought these biscuits were sugar-free, but they ___________ .
5. They said she was getting better, but she ___________ .
6. I'll be moving to London, but my girlfriend ___________ .
7. My husband's going to the wedding, but I ___________ .
8. Jo likes Indian food, but Andrew ___________ .
9. Bill thought I'd forgotten our wedding anniversary, but I ___________ .
10. The bedroom's been decorated, but the bathroom ___________ .
11. He said that he was really sorry, but he ___________ .
12. We thought that we were doing it correctly, but we ___________ .

5 Negative questions

Match a question in **A** with a line in **B**.

A	B
1 Don't you want me to help you? 2 Do you want me to help you?	a I thought you did. b I will if you want.
3 Aren't you a member of the tennis club? 4 Are you a member of the tennis club?	c I'm sure I've seen you there. d If you are, we could have a game.
5 Don't you know the answer? 6 Do you know the answer?	e Yes or no? f I'm surprised at you!
7 Don't you think it's beautiful? 8 Do you think it's beautiful?	g Surely you agree with me! h I'm asking because I'm not sure.
9 Didn't I tell you I'm going out tonight? 10 Did I tell you I'm going out tonight?	i I can't remember now. j I thought I had. Sorry!

6 *no, not, -n't,* or *none*?

Complete the sentences with *no*, *not*, *-n't*, or *none*.

1 I'll help you, but __________ tonight.

2 We have __________ onions left. Sorry!

3 __________ of us understood the lesson.

4 The teacher was __________ very clear.

5 I asked you __________ to make a mess.

6 Why did __________ you do what I asked?

7 How do you manage __________ to put on any weight?

8 Bring Alessia to the party, but __________ Ben. He's too loud.

9 There's __________ meat in this dish, so it's suitable for vegetarians.

10 **A** Who likes chemistry?
B __________ me.

11 **A** Where's the nearest swimming pool?
B There are __________ around here.

12 She has __________ idea of how to enjoy herself.

13 Why have __________ you emailed me for so long?

14 I can play the piano a little bit, but __________ properly.

15 **A** Do you work late?
B __________ if I can help it.

16 **A** Where's the coffee?
B There's __________ left.

17 The management accepts __________ responsibility for items left in the cloakroom.

18 I've got __________ time for people who are rude.

19 __________ of my friends smoke.

20 **A** Do you like jazz?
B __________ usually.

"Didn't you get the email?"

7 I don't think you're right

1 In English, we usually say *I don't think* + affirmative verb:

*I **don't think I know** you.* NOT ~~I think I don't~~ know you.

We do the same with *believe*, *suppose*, and *expect*.

*I **don't expect** we'**ll meet** again.*

*My friends **didn't believe** I'**d do** a bungee jump!*

2 We can also use *seem*, *expect*, and *want* with the negative (+ object) + infinitive:

*She **doesn't** seem **to be** very happy.*

*I **don't** expect **to get** the job.*

*I **don't** want **to go back** to that restaurant.*

*He **doesn't** expect **us to pass** the exams.*

Rewrite the sentences, using the verb in brackets in the negative.

1 You haven't met my wife. (think)

I don't think you've met my wife.

2 You haven't got change for a 20-euro note. (suppose)

I ______________________________.

3 This machine isn't working. (seem)

This machine ______________________________.

4 It wasn't going to rain. (think)

I ______________________________.

5 Their daughter's moving to Canada. They aren't happy. (want)

They ______________________________.

6 I'm surprised to see you here. (expect)

I ______________________________.

7 You haven't seen Robert recently. (suppose)

I ______________________________.

8 I wouldn't like snails. (think)

I ______________________________.

9 You probably don't remember me. (expect)

I ______________________________.

10 She didn't pass all her exams. (believe)

I ______________________________.

8 Not the whole truth!

White lies are what we say to people so as not to upset them or to get out of an awkward situation.

1 Listen and match the conversations with the pictures.

A

B

C

D

E

F

G

H

2 Now match the pictures (A–H) to what the people are really thinking.

1 [H] Only 100 mph! Actually, it was 110.

2 [ ] Really? You look 40-plus!

3 [ ] I went for a drink with friends from work.

4 [ ] That dress is too tight for you.

5 [ ] What a boring present!

6 [ ] Oh help! My mouth is on fire!

7 [ ] Great! I managed to get away without paying.

8 [ ] What an ugly baby!

Prepositions

9 Verb + preposition

Many verbs are followed by prepositions. Complete the sentences with the correct preposition.

1 I agree *with* every word you say.
2 I applied __________ the job, but I didn't get it.
3 He died __________ a heart attack.
4 She's suffering __________ a nasty chest infection.
5 Do you believe __________ magic?
6 I didn't realize Maria was married __________ George.
7 Don't you think Mike's been acting __________ a very strange way?
8 Did you succeed __________ convincing your father you were telling the truth?
9 Compared __________ you, I'm not very intelligent at all!
10 We've complained __________ our teacher __________ the amount of homework we get.
11 Stop laughing __________ me. It isn't funny!
12 I've completely fallen __________ love __________ you.
13 Who will you vote __________ in the next election?
14 Bollywood sensation Katrina Kaif has appeared __________ over 30 films.

Vocabulary

10 Antonyms and synonyms

1 For the words in **A**, write their opposites in **B**, using prefixes.

A	B	C
Adjectives		
real	*unreal*	*fake*
truthful		
credible		
plausible		
probable		
pleased		
normal		
professional		
important		
Nouns		
honesty		
reality		
belief		
Verbs		
appear		
understand		
trust		
cover		

2 In column **C**, write synonyms for the words in **B**, using the words in the box.

~~fake~~	confuse	dishonest	reveal
deceit	unbelievable	fantasy	vanish
ridiculous	annoyed	bizarre	amateur
unlikely	trivial	incredulity	suspect

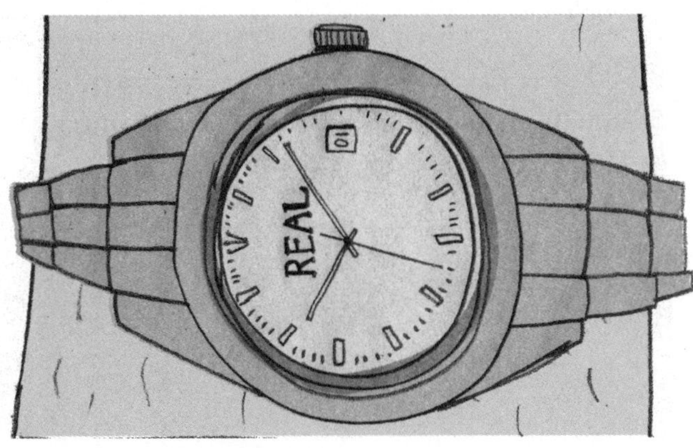

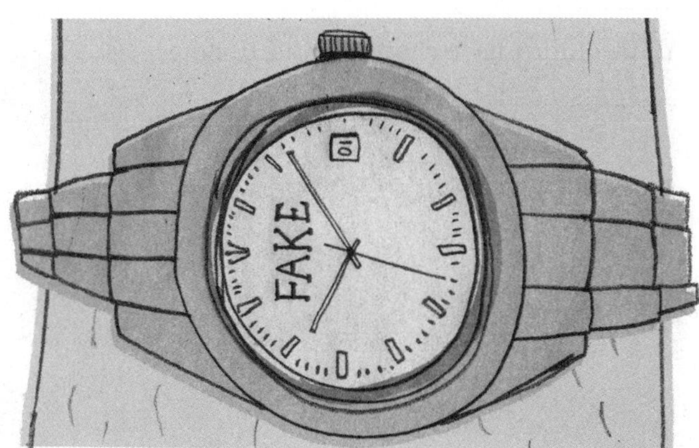

Pronunciation

11 Intonation in question tags

In question tags the intonation either falls ↘ or rises ↗.

1 ↘ Falling intonation means that the sentence is more like a statement = 'I'm sure I'm right. Can you just confirm this for me?'

2 ↗ Rising intonation means that the sentence is more like a real question = 'I'm not sure if I'm right about this. Correct me if I'm wrong.'

You've lost the car keys again, haven't you?

You've been invited to Jane's party, haven't you?

Both patterns are very common in spoken English because they invite other people to join in the conversation.

1 Write the question tags for the statements. Mark whether it falls or rises.

1 It's really warm again today, ↘ isn't it ?
2 You're angry with me, __________ ?
3 Last night was such a hot night, __________ ?
4 You couldn't help me carry this bag, __________ ?
5 Antonio's late again, __________ ?
6 It's cold for this time of year, __________ ?
7 John didn't fail his driving test again, __________ ?
8 You haven't seen my pen anywhere, __________ ?
9 By the end of the film we were all in tears, __________ ?
10 You wouldn't have change for a £10 note, __________ ?

2 Write a sentence and a question tag for these situations and mark the intonation pattern.

1 You ask Tom if he could help you do your homework.
Tom, you couldn't help me with my homework, could you? ↗
2 You're coming out of a restaurant where you have just had a really tasteless meal with a friend.
That ____________________ ?
3 You can't believe that your sister has borrowed your new coat again.
You ____________________ ?
4 You need a neighbour to water your plants while you're away.
You ____________________ ?
5 You think that Vanessa is going on a business trip to Rome next week, but you're not sure.
Vanessa, you ____________________ ?

Future forms • Conjunctions in time clauses
• Commonly confused words • Phrasal verbs – types 2 and 3
• Sounds and spelling

Looking ahead

Future forms

1 Question tags

Match a sentence in **A** with a question tag in **B**.

A	B
1 You're going to work harder from now on,	will we?
2 I'll see you next week,	doesn't it?
3 Kate's leaving soon,	won't we?
4 You'll ring when you get there,	are you?
5 Our plane takes off at 4 p.m.,	won't I?
6 The painters will have finished by next week,	isn't she?
7 You aren't getting married next week,	won't you?
8 We won't need tickets to get in,	won't they?
9 We'll be millionaires one day,	will he?
10 Max won't be coming,	aren't you?

"I just have a feeling that my son is not going to grow up to be a farmer."

2 *will* or *going to*?

Complete the conversations with *will* or *going to* in the correct form. Sometimes there is more than one answer.

1 **A** I __________ make myself a sandwich. Do you want one?
B No, thanks. I __________ have something later.

2 **A** Marco and Lia __________ spend their honeymoon in Venice.
B How wonderful! I'm sure they __________ love it!

3 **A** Bye, Mum. I __________ meet Tom and Mel. I __________ be back at about ten o'clock.
B OK, but don't be late again or I __________ be really annoyed.

4 **A** Jo __________ be furious when she finds out I've crashed the car.
B She __________ understand if you explain that it wasn't your fault.

5 **A** I've just seen the weather forecast and it __________ be chilly again.
B I think I __________ take a coat then.

6 **A** I'm tired. I think I __________ go to bed.
B I __________ watch the news, then I __________ join you.

7 **A** My boss has told me I __________ be promoted.
B Congratulations! We __________ have to celebrate!

8 **A** Mr Smith, now you've won the lottery you __________ be the fifth-richest man in England. How do you feel about that?
B I __________ tell you next week. I'm too shocked at the moment!

3 What does John say?

Write what John actually says in these situations. Use a future form.

1 He sees some very black clouds in the sky.
   It's going to rain.

2 His sister has just reminded him that it is his grandmother's birthday soon.
   I ________________________.

3 He has decided to study hard for his final exams.
   I ________________________.

4 He's made an appointment to see the dentist next Friday.
   I ________________________.

5 He predicts a win for his team, Manchester United, on Saturday.
   I think ________________________.

6 He's stuck in a traffic jam. He's late for a meeting. He rings his office.
   I'm sorry. ________________________.

7 His sister is pregnant. The baby is due next March.
   My sister ________________________.

8 His plane ticket for next Sunday says: Departure 7.30 a.m. London, Heathrow.
   My plane ________________________.

9 He can see himself lying on a beach in Spain next week at this time.
   This time next week ________________________.

10 He predicts hot weather there.
   I think it ________________________.

4 Future Continuous or Future Perfect? By the time I'm 30 ...

1 Listen to Tommy (**T**), Jack (**J**), and Millie (**M**) talking about their futures. Who wants to …

become a pilot? *T*	win an Olympic medal?
work in the US?	mix with celebrities?
live in the north of England?	design swimwear?
move to London?	marry a film star?
travel the world?	live near the river?
study law?	buy a penthouse flat?
buy a farm?	go clubbing and partying?

2 Listen again and complete the sentences about what Tommy, Jack, and Millie will have done or will be doing by the time they are 30.

By the time Tommy is 30, …

1 *he'll be flying for British Airways.*
2 *he will have moved to London.*
3 ________________
4 ________________
5 ________________

By the time Jack is 30, …

1 *he* ________________
2 ________________
3 ________________
4 ________________

By the time Millie is 30, …

1 *she* ________________
2 ________________
3 ________________
4 ________________

5 An inspirational teenager

Read the interview and circle the best future form.

Dreams Can Come True
Meet Noah Grey, a young gymnast with high aspirations for the next Olympics.

I Hello, Noah. It is good of you to be interviewed today, as I know you have a busy training schedule.

N That's OK. I [1] *'ll take / 'm taking* a couple of days off anyway as it's my birthday tomorrow. I [2] *'m / 'm going to be* 18 – an adult at last.

I Only 18 and you've accomplished so much already! You won a bronze medal at the European Championships last year, and I know you [3] *'ll be hoping / 'll have hoped* to win gold at the next Olympics.

N That's my dream. I [4] *'ll never give up / 'll never be giving up* until I've done all I can to achieve it. That's what keeps me going through the hours of training. I keep telling myself it'll be worth it if I [5] *win / will win* gold. Failure isn't an option.

I You're very tough on yourself, Noah. That's a lot of commitment and hard work. You're still young. Surely you must spend time with friends.

N No, gymnastics is everything to me. I [6] *'ll be training / 'll have been training* intensively for six years by the next Olympics, and every minute of practice will help.

I The World Championships [7] *are being staged / are staged* in China next year. How are you preparing for this competition?

N Well, I'm good at the pommel horse and the parallel bars, so by the time the Championships start, I [8] *concentrate / 'll have concentrated* on them most. I think the bars [9] *will be / are being* my best event.

I Will you [10] *be hoping / have hoped* for a medal?

N Yes, I [11] *will / have*. Maybe silver or bronze.

I You're such a role model for young people today. Do you have any advice for other young hopefuls?

N Yes, never lose sight of your dream. If you work hard, you [12] *will have been / will be* successful.

I Thank you, Noah. I wish you all the best and Happy Birthday for tomorrow.

Conjunctions in time clauses

6 Future time clauses

1 Notice that in clauses after *if*, *when*, *as soon as*, *until*, *before*, *after*, *once*, and *unless*, we normally use a present tense to talk about the future. A future form is not used.

I'll phone you ***when I arrive***. NOT *when I'll arrive*

I won't marry you ***unless you give up*** *smoking!*
NOT *unless you'll give up*

2 To show that the first action will be completed before the second, we use the Present Perfect.

I'll fax you the report ***as soon as I've written it***.

They're going to emigrate to Australia ***after the baby has been born***.

Complete the sentences with the verbs in brackets in the correct tense.

1 Unless you __________ (eat) something, you __________ (not get) better.

2 We __________ (not move) to Paris until we __________ (find) a flat there to rent.

3 You __________ (love) Adam when you __________ (meet) him. He's so funny.

4 _____ you __________ (learn) to drive as soon as you __________ (be) 17?

5 The children __________ (not go) to bed unless they __________ (have) a glass of milk.

6 It __________ (be) at least an hour before I __________ (finish) this report.

7 If you __________ (not do) well in the test, _____ you __________ (have to) do it again?

8 As soon as we __________ (be) able to process the information, we __________ (deal) with your request.

9 The doctor says that I __________ (feel) much better once I __________ (have) the operation.

10 Once you __________ (try) 'Glowhite' toothpaste, you __________ (never use) anything else!

7 Check it

In these conversations, some of the future forms are wrong. Find the mistakes and correct them.

1 ☑ **A** Have you heard? Sue's going to have a baby.
☐ **B** Really? ~~I'm going to~~ I'll give her a ring this evening to congratulate her.

2 ☐ **A** What do you do this weekend?
☐ **B** I don't know yet. Maybe I'll give Paul a ring and see what he's doing.

3 ☐ **A** I'll be honest with you, Matthew. I don't think you're going to pass this exam.
☐ **B** Oh, no! What will I be doing?

4 ☐ **A** Is it true that Rachel will go to the States to work as a nanny?
☐ **B** Yes, and guess what! I am, too!

5 ☐ **A** Our plane leaves at six o'clock on Saturday morning.
☐ **B** You have to wake me up. I can never get up in the mornings.

6 ☐ **A** It's my birthday tomorrow. I'm going to be 30!
☐ **B** 30! That's ancient! You are getting your pension soon.

7 ☐ **A** My parents will be arriving soon, and the house looks like a pigsty.
☐ **B** Don't worry. It'll only be taking a few minutes to clear up.

8 ☐ **A** Will you be going skiing as usual after Christmas?
☐ **B** Not this year. It's just too expensive. We'll stay at home.

9 ☐ **A** I'll ring you as soon as I'll arrive.
☐ **B** Please do. We'll be waiting to hear you've arrived safely.

10 ☐ **A** Are you going to Sam's party on Friday?
☐ **B** Yeah, unless I am getting held up at work.

Vocabulary

8 Hot verbs – *take, put*

Complete the conversation between Kerry and Daisy with the correct form of *take* or *put*.

K Hi, Kerry. Are you thinking of [1] __________ part in that acting competition? Second prize is tickets for Emma Watson's new film. You're a big fan of hers, aren't you?

D She's my heroine. I think she's just brilliant. If she [2] __________ her mind to it, she can do anything.

K Aren't you [3] __________ her on a pedestal? She was OK in the Harry Potter films, but she's not that great.

D What! She's done so much more than Harry Potter. She [4] __________ up modelling and won a People's Choice award for her latest film.

K Pretty impressive stuff, I suppose. Isn't she studying as well?

D She certainly is. She [5] __________ some time off university to promote her films, but she's back there now and finishing her degree.

K OK, sorry – I [6] __________ back what I said. It's not fair, is it? Some people have all the luck.

D Come on! You've been offered a good part in *Shrek the Musical*. I think your acting career is about to [7] __________ off!

K It's not a very big part. I'm just in the chorus.

D Don't [8] __________ yourself down. If you [9] __________ in enough effort, you'll become a star. You've got a great singing voice, too.

K Oh Daisy, do you really think so?

D Yeah, I do. Our music coach has really [10] __________ to you. She thinks you've got real promise. You'll be famous one day.

K We both will! Come on! Let's [11] __________ our names down for this competition.

D And if one of us wins, they'll have to [12] __________ the other out for a meal.

K Deal!

Listen and check.

9 Commonly confused words

Complete the sentences using the words in the box in the correct form.

expect wait for look forward to

1 a We __________ the rain to stop so that we can play tennis.
  b The weather forecast says a lot of rain __________ over the next few days.
  c I'm very excited. I'm __________ starting my new job at the bank.

pass spend waste

2 a I __________ too much time with my mates and not enough time with my girlfriend.
  b I usually read the newspaper to __________ the time on train journeys.
  c I __________ my time at school. I wish I'd tried harder and studied more.

see watch look at

3 a _____ you _____ that new Spielberg film yet?
  b The police sat in their car. They __________ every move the men made.
  c __________ this picture little Amy has painted!

actually at the moment really

4 a **A** What a shame James lost the match!
    B __________ , he won.
  b The kids are playing in the garden __________ .
  c Love that dress. You __________ look wonderful!

lend borrow owe

5 a I have a student loan. I __________ the bank £10,000, which is a big debt.
  b Jed __________ £5,000 from the bank to buy a car.
  c Could you __________ me £20 until the end of the week? I'm broke.

angry nervous embarrassed

6 a He felt __________ when he realized that he couldn't remember her name.
  b I'm very __________ about my interview tomorrow.
  c We're __________ with the government for not listening to us.

Phrasal verbs

10 Type 2 and type 3

Type 2 and type 3 phrasal verbs have an object and a particle.

Type 2

The particle can move position. NOTE A particle always comes after pronouns (*him, it, me, etc.*).

__Take off__ your coat. __Take__ your coat __off__.
__Take__ it __off__. NOT ~~Take off it~~.

I __put on__ the DVD. I __put__ the DVD __on__.
I __put__ it __on__. NOT ~~I put on it~~.

Type 3

The particle cannot move.

__Look after__ your sister.
NOT ~~Look your sister after~~.
~~Look her after~~.

I'll __look into__ the problem.
NOT ~~I'll look the problem into~~.
~~I'll look it into.~~

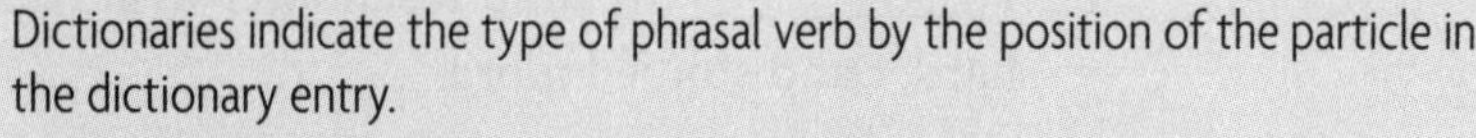

Dictionaries indicate the type of phrasal verb by the position of the particle in the dictionary entry.

put sth on The particle is shown *after* **sth**. (Type 2)

look into sth The particle is shown *before* **sth**. (Type 3)

Put a pronoun in the correct place in these sentences.

1 Listen to this song. I'll put _it_ on _-_ for you.
2 I know you've got a lot of problems, but I'm sure you'll get _-_ through _them_ .
3 I can't remember the directions. I couldn't take ___________ all in ___________ .
4 There's a problem with my computer. I'll sort ___________ out ___________ tomorrow.
5 We're having a meeting on the 25th. Put ___________ in ___________ your diary.
6 There are clothes all over your bedroom. Please put ___________ away ___________ .
7 If you're going out with your little brother, you'd better look ___________ after ___________ .
8 I'm sorry you had a complaint about your room. I'll look ___________ into ___________ right away.
9 That was a mean thing you said! Take ___________ back ___________ !
10 I liked Ann, but since you told me what she did, you've put me ___________ off ___________ .

Pronunciation

11 Sounds and spelling

1 Listen and match the letters underlined in each word with the correct sound.

1	won't	/ʌ/	/əʊ/	/ɒ/
2	walk	/ɔː/	/ɑː/	/ɒ/
3	wonder	/ʌ/	/ɔː/	/ɒ/
4	woman	/ʊ/	/əʊ/	/ʌ/
5	warm	/ɔː/	/aɪ/	/ɜː/
6	word	/ɔː/	/ɜː/	/aɪ/
7	wear	/eə/	/e/	/iː/
8	weight	/aɪ/	/eɪ/	/e/
9	want	/æ/	/əʊ/	/ɒ/
10	work	/ɔː/	/ɜː/	/ɔɪ/
11	wander	/ʌ/	/ɔː/	/ɒ/
12	women	/ʊ/	/əʊ/	/ɪ/
13	worm	/ɔː/	/ɔɪ/	/ɜː/
14	ward	/ɑː/	/aɪ/	/ɔː/
15	weary	/eə/	/ɪə/	/iː/
16	weird	/aɪ/	/eɪ/	/ɪə/

2 In each group of words, three words rhyme. Circle the odd one out.

1	/ʌ/	done	phone	won	son
2	/ʊ/	would	should	good	blood
3	/uː/	move	love	prove	groove
4	/əʊ/	though	through	throw	sew
5	/eɪ/	weak	break	ache	shake
6	/aʊ/	flower	power	tower	lower
7	/ɜː/	worth	birth	north	earth
8	/eɪ/	hate	wait	weight	height
9	/ɪə/	fear	near	pear	clear
10	/eə/	share	bear	fair	hear

Countable and uncountable nouns • Expressing quantity • Compounds with *some*, *any*, *no*, *every* • Money • Prepositions • Words with variable stress

Hitting the big time

Countable and uncountable nouns

1 Countable or uncountable?

Circle the noun in each group that is uncountable.

1 cheque coin cash salary bonus

2 job employee boss unemployment profession

3 motorway traffic traffic jam hold-up rush hour

4 holiday journey flight luggage suitcase

5 meal dish food menu dessert

6 pop group musical music opera concert

7 arrest violence accident crime criminal

Circle the noun in each group that is usually countable.

8 luck happiness opportunity fun help

9 ingredient cutlery fruit meat food

10 fresh air sleep fluid health energy

2 *some* or *any*?

Complete the sentences with *some* or *any*.

1 Why don't you ask your father to lend you ______ money? I haven't got ______ .

2 ______ people don't have ______ problems learning foreign languages.

3 Would you like ______ more fizzy mineral water?

I don't want ______ more.

4 My teenage sister never has ______ difficulty learning the words of the latest pop songs. There are hardly ______ she doesn't know by heart.

5 I didn't realize that there was still ______ coffee left. I've made ______ more.

6 I did this exercise without ______ help.

3 *much* or *many*?

Rewrite the sentences using the words in brackets and *much* or *many*. Make any other necessary changes.

1 I'm not sure how much drink to buy. (cans of cola)

I'm not sure how many cans of cola to buy.

2 Are there many jobs to be done in the garden? (work)

____

3 I didn't spend many hours on the homework. (time)

____

4 Did they do many experiments before they found a cure? (research)

____

5 I didn't have too much difficulty with this exercise either. (problems)

____

6 I've got too many suitcases. I can't carry them all. (luggage)

____

7 There are too many cars and lorries on the streets of our town. (traffic)

____

8 They couldn't give me many details about the delay to our flight. (information)

____

4 The canteen

1 Look at the picture of the students' canteen. Write ten sentences, using each expression in the box once.

several   a couple of   a few   not much   lots of not many   a little   hardly any   no   a huge amount of

1 ______
2 ______
3 ______
4 ______
5 ______
6 ______
7 ______
8 ______
9 ______
10 ______

2 Answer the students' questions, using an expression of quantity without a noun.

1 Is there any chocolate cake?
Sorry, there's *none* left.

2 What about rice?
Well, there's *a little* .

3 Can I have some spaghetti?
Yes, of course, there's ______ left.

4 Have you got lots of tuna sandwiches?
Well, there are ______ .

5 Two vegetable curries, please.
Sorry, there's ______ left.

6 Can I have some chips with my burger?
Sorry, there are ______ left.

7 Have you got apple pie today?
Yes, just ______ .

8 Are there any chocolate biscuits?
Well, there are ______ .

9 Can I have a large portion of fruit salad, please?
Sorry, there's only ______ left.

10 Have you run out of bananas?
No, I think we've got ______ out the back.

11 **A** Is this all the apple juice you've got?
B Yes, I'm afraid there are only ______ cartons left.
A OK, I'll take those, and three of orange juice, please.
B No problem, we've got ______ of orange.

5 *very little, a little, very few, a few, fewer, less*

Rewrite the sentences with *very little*, *a little*, *very few*, *a few*, *fewer*, or *less*. Change all the underlined words.

1 There was a lot of wine at the party, but hardly any was drunk. *very little*

2 I'm on a diet so I'll just have three crackers and a small piece of cheese.

3 Children don't have as much respect as they used to for their teachers.

4 Lots of people have tried to climb Everest, but not many have succeeded.

5 Dave can speak fluent Norwegian and some Swedish.

6 Not as many people smoke these days.

7 Not many people manage to become completely fluent in a language.

8 It's been three or four years since we last saw him.

9 There isn't very much I can do to help you.

10 There are lots of reasons why I don't want to expand the business. Here are some of them.

Compounds with *some*, *any*, *no*, *every*

6 *something, anybody, nowhere, everyone ...*

1 *Any, anyone, anybody, anywhere*, and *anything* can mean it doesn't matter which/who/where/what.

Put the picture ***anywhere****, I don't mind.*
You can say ***anything*** *you want. I don't care.*
Borrow ***any*** *book you want.*

2 *Everybody* and *everything* are singular, not plural.
Everybody *knows who did it.*

Everyone *likes John.*

1 Complete the sentences with a combination of these words.

some / any / no / every	+	one / body / thing / where

1 I don't care where we go on holiday as long as it's __________ hot.
2 Does __________ want a cup of tea?
3 I've looked for my contact lens, but I can't find it __________ .
4 **A** What do you want for dinner, Harry?
B Oh, __________ , I don't mind!
5 This sale is fantastic. There's 50% off __________ in the shop.
6 It's really boring at Auntie Martha's, there's absolutely __________ to do.
7 I'm a very sensitive person. __________ understands me.
8 There was __________ for me to sit on the train so I had to stand.
9 Jane's getting engaged to __________ she met on holiday.
10 Sue is such a chatterbox; she's always got __________ to say, but she never says __________ interesting.
11 Our dog will go for a walk with __________ .
12 Tommy's so popular. __________ likes him.

2 Match a line in **A** with a line in **B** to make sentences.

A	B
1 He told them he knew 2 He didn't tell them	a anything. b nothing.
3 I think they live 4 I don't mind. I'll live	c somewhere near here. d anywhere near here.
5 Anybody 6 Nobody	e phoned you. Sorry! f can cook. It's easy.
7 I've searched 8 I can't find it	g anywhere. h everywhere.
9 I thought I'd know 10 I didn't know	i somebody at the party. j anyone at the party.
11 My parents never took me 12 My parents took me	k everywhere. l anywhere.
13 Jane always got 14 Jane didn't have	m everything she wanted. n anything to wear.
15 I've already had 16 I've had	o something to eat. p nothing to eat.

Expressing quantity

7 If at first you don't succeed

Read about three entrepreneurs. Complete their stories using the words in the boxes.

If at first you don't succeed ...

In reality TV programme *Dragons' Den*, hopeful entrepreneurs pitch their business ideas to a panel of multi-millionaires. The 'Dragons' invest if they believe the business is viable. But sometimes they are wrong ...

The Trunki

any	a bit	all	few
many	one piece	one of	

The Trunki is a colourful, adaptable piece of hand luggage for children which 1 ______ of us will have seen at airports. It is a small suitcase with wheels, which can be used as a seat for children who are getting 2 ______ tired, or easily pulled by a parent with a small child sitting on top. The Trunki is a great invention and 3 ______ parents travelling by plane with young children would disagree.
Despite its obvious potential, the inventor of the Trunki, Rob Law, was dismissed from the Den without 4 ______ financial backing.
The Trunki is now 5 ______ the top-selling baggage items at department stores in the UK.
Rob offers 6 ______ new entrepreneurs 7 ______ of advice:
'If at first you don't succeed, try, try, try again.'

The SwimFin

hundred	a couple	all
anything	more	
something	nobody	

Kevin Moseley is an inventor with a sense of humour. He came up with the idea of designing a

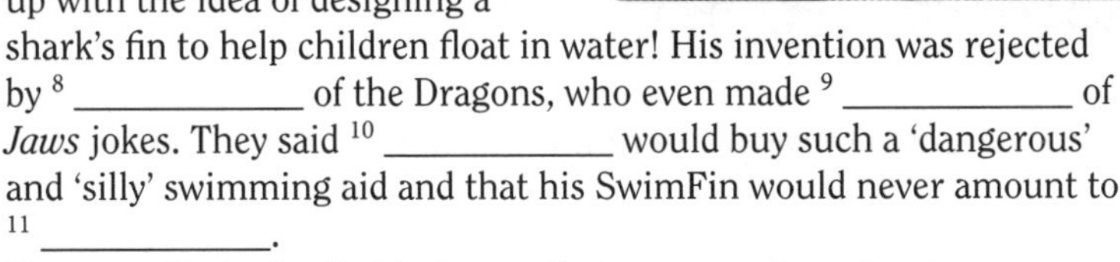

shark's fin to help children float in water! His invention was rejected by 8 ______ of the Dragons, who even made 9 ______ of *Jaws* jokes. They said 10 ______ would buy such a 'dangerous' and 'silly' swimming aid and that his SwimFin would never amount to 11 ______.
However, Kevin decided to ignore their comments and make 12 ______ SwimFins in his garage. Two years later, the SwimFin is a 13 ______-thousand pound business and a worldwide success, 14 ______ the Dragons hadn't anticipated!

Destination London

any	a great deal	none	several
everything	no one	more than	

15 ______ is a better example of never giving up than Rachel Lowe. She took her Destination London board game to the Den where she was subjected to 16 ______ of ridicule from the Dragons. 17 ______ of them saw a future in the game, and she left without 18 ______ investment.
However, Rachel had the last laugh when 19 ______ months later Destination London sold 20 ______ any other toy at the world-famous toy store, Hamleys. The Destination brand now comprises over 20 editions, including a Harry Potter version.
Unfortunately, because of the banking crises, Rachel's company went into administration, and she lost 21 ______ . Rachel never gave up, though, and launched a new fragrance and accessories brand, 'She Who Dares'.

Vocabulary

8 Money advice

1 Read the advice on how to manage your money. Complete 1–8 with verbs from the box.

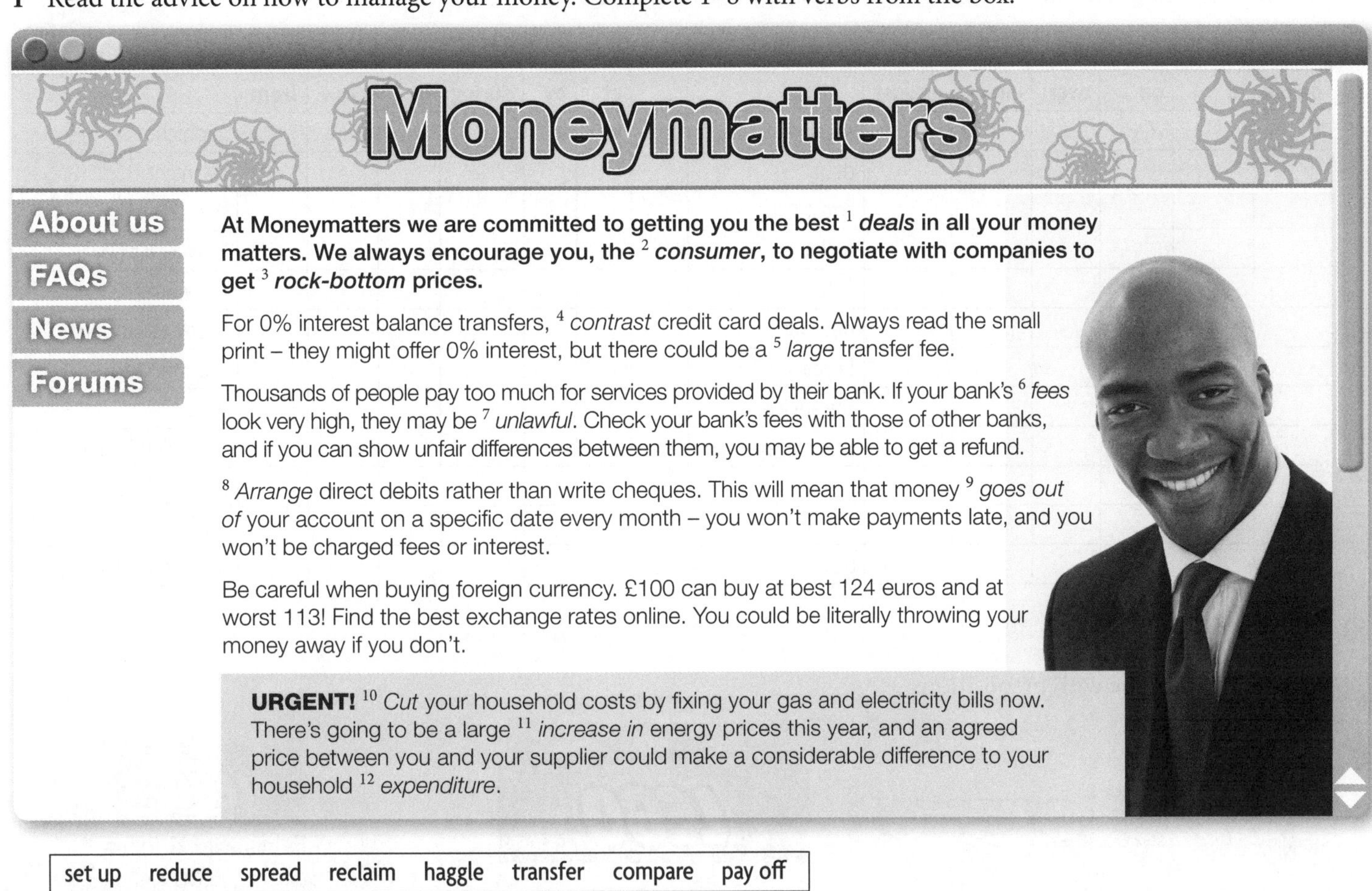
Moneymatters
About us
FAQs
News
Forums
At Moneymatters we are committed to getting you the best [1] *deals* in all your money matters. We always encourage you, the [2] *consumer*, to negotiate with companies to get [3] *rock-bottom* prices.
For 0% interest balance transfers, [4] *contrast* credit card deals. Always read the small print – they might offer 0% interest, but there could be a [5] *large* transfer fee.
Thousands of people pay too much for services provided by their bank. If your bank's [6] *fees* look very high, they may be [7] *unlawful*. Check your bank's fees with those of other banks, and if you can show unfair differences between them, you may be able to get a refund.
[8] *Arrange* direct debits rather than write cheques. This will mean that money [9] *goes out of* your account on a specific date every month – you won't make payments late, and you won't be charged fees or interest.
Be careful when buying foreign currency. £100 can buy at best 124 euros and at worst 113! Find the best exchange rates online. You could be literally throwing your money away if you don't.
URGENT! [10] *Cut* your household costs by fixing your gas and electricity bills now. There's going to be a large [11] *increase in* energy prices this year, and an agreed price between you and your supplier could make a considerable difference to your household [12] *expenditure*.

set up	reduce	spread	reclaim	haggle	transfer	compare	pay off

1 You can ___________ your heating bill by up to 20% by insulating your loft.

2 You should ___________ your credit card balance to a new card with 0% interest.

3 You can ___________ unfair bank charges by contacting your bank directly.

4 Before renewing your car insurance, go online and ___________ prices. You could be paying far too much!

5 You should always ___________ over your mobile phone package, you can usually negotiate a better deal!

6 Rather than paying in full, ___________ the cost of household bills over the year in monthly or quarterly payments.

7 To manage your finances more efficiently, ___________ direct debits, then you know exactly when money is leaving your bank account.

8 It is always advisable to ___________ credit card balances in full each month to avoid paying high interest charges.

2 Read the text again. Which words from the box can replace the words in *italics*?

customer ☐	hefty ☐	hike ☐	charges ☐	set up ☐	leaves ☐
bargains ☐	slash ☐	the lowest ☐	compare ☐	illegal ☐	outgoings ☐

Prepositions

9 Prepositions and nouns that go together

Which prepositions go with the words on the right in these two tables?

A						
below	**in**	**on**	**over**	**under**	**against**	
✓		✓				average
						debt
						arrest
						Arabic
						75%
						freezing
						18 years old
						the advice
						new management
						holiday
						pressure
						business

B						
at	**by**	**during**	**in**	**on**	**from**	
✓	✓					midnight
						the night
						the beginning
						New Year's Day
						the winter
						Friday afternoon
						the weekend
						time
						a fortnight's time
						the rush hour
						his forties
						the end of the week

10 Prepositions in context

Complete the article with prepositions.

The Story of LEGO

The world-famous LEGO company has its origins in the workshop of a poor Danish carpenter, Ole Kirk Christiansen [1] ______ the first half of the 20th century. [2] ______ these humble beginnings, it has grown to become one of the most popular toys [3] ______ all time.

Ole, the tenth son in the family, earned a living making toys with his father. Finally, he became a master carpenter and [4] ______ 1932 he set up his own business making toys and wooden bricks. He called the company LEGO, which means 'play well' [5] ______ Danish. Unfortunately, ten years later his factory burned down. However, despite being [6] ______ great financial pressure, Ole had it rebuilt. This took three years and [7] ______ that time he learnt of a British company which specialized [8] ______ plastic moulding machines. His managers thought they were too expensive, but [9] ______ their advice, Ole bought one. It was worth the investment. [10] ______ the end of the decade, the company was producing a successful range of toys and interlocking bricks, and Ole's son, Godtfred, had joined him [11] ______ the business.

Sadly, Ole didn't live to see the success of his company. He died [12] ______ the age of 66 and Godtfred became Managing Director. The modern brick design was patented [13] ______ 28 January 1958, and bricks from that year are still compatible [14] ______ bricks today.

Unbelievably, [15] ______ the 1960s, the LEGO factory was struck [16] ______ lightning and burned [17] ______ the ground again. After this, Godtfred had to rethink the direction of the company. This time, [18] ______ the advice of his directors, he decided to concentrate solely [19] ______ the hugely successful interlocking plastic bricks.

Godtfred's son, Kjeld, is the current Deputy-Chairman and to celebrate the company's 80th anniversary, a short animated film called 'The LEGO story' was released [20] ______ August 2012.

Facts and figures

1. Today, the LEGO club has 4.7 million members worldwide.
2. On average, every person on Earth owns 86 LEGO bricks.
3. A column of 40 billion LEGO bricks would reach the moon.
4. Ten LEGO sets are sold every second.
5. The number of bricks sold yearly would go 18 times round the world.

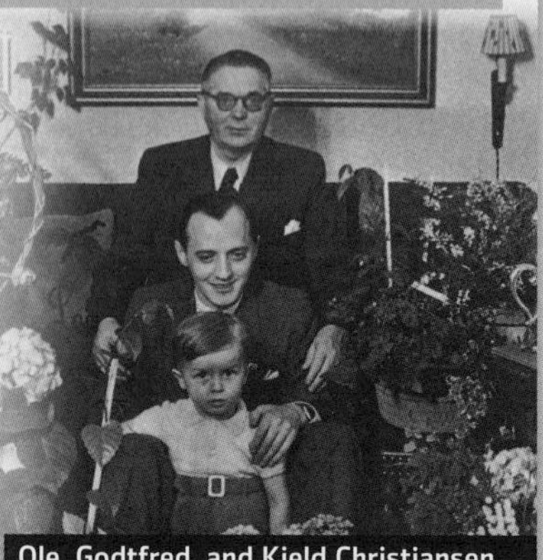

Ole, Godtfred, and Kjeld Christiansen, three generations of LEGO men.

Listening

11 A job interview

1 Listen to the interview. Which job is Jane going for?

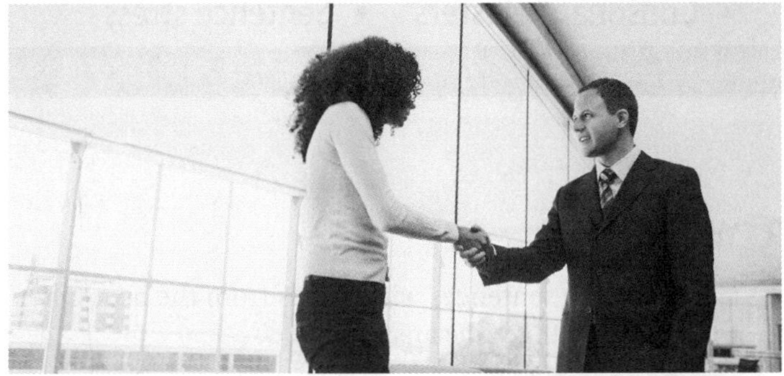

WANTED

A motivated and enthusiastic sales person to sell Commodore cosmetics at our beauty department at Selfridges, London. Minimum two years' experience in cosmetic sales.

RECEPTIONIST

A business-focused receptionist needed for a busy law office in central Bristol. Experience desirable. Immediate start required.

SALES REPRESENTATIVE

Full-time sales representative needed for South West region. A proven track-record in sales essential. Knowledge of UK pet market desirable.

2 Listen again and complete the sentences.

1. No, I live near Bristol so it was __________ 30 minutes …
2. Do you know __________ about our company?
3. … and you are __________ pet food companies …
4. … and is a market bestseller endorsed by __________ high-profile celebrity pet owners.
5. You seem to know __________ about our company.
6. Could you give me __________ information on your key skills …
7. … I was always able to work on my own __________ guidance.
8. I used to feel anxious about giving presentations to __________ people …
9. … been on __________ courses which have made a huge difference.

Pronunciation

12 Words with variable stress

1 Listen to the pronunciation of the words. Write **N** for noun and **V** for verb.

1 ☐	refuse	7 ☐	permit
2 ☐	transport	8 ☐	record
3 ☐	produce	9 ☐	contract
4 ☐	decrease	10 ☐	desert
5 ☐	progress	11 ☐	present
6 ☐	insult	12 ☐	content

2 Read this news item aloud. Pay attention to the shifting stress on words that are both verbs and nouns.

'Good evening. Here is the news. Oil imports continued to increase in the last quarter. The cost of transport fuel is already at record levels, and the Prime Minister refuses to rule out further increases. Members of the Transport Workers' Union insist that they will protest against any future price rises. They presented a report maintaining that present fuel price increases are due to a decrease in investment in railway transport by the government.'

Listen and check. Practise reading the text again.

3 Read this news item and mark the stress on the words in **bold**. Then read it aloud, paying attention to the shifting stress.

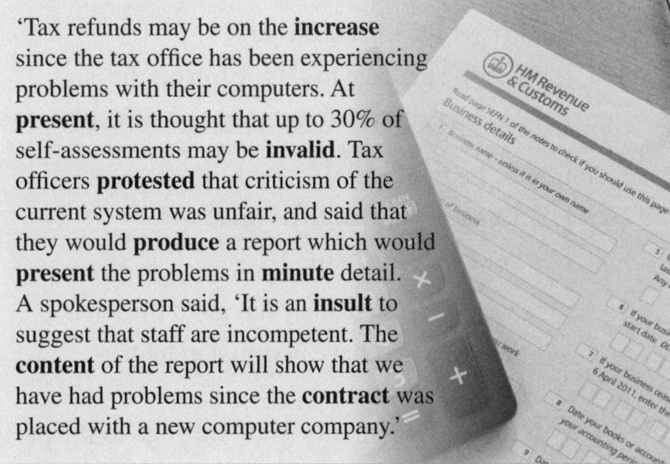

'Tax refunds may be on the **increase** since the tax office has been experiencing problems with their computers. At **present**, it is thought that up to 30% of self-assessments may be **invalid**. Tax officers **protested** that criticism of the current system was unfair, and said that they would **produce** a report which would **present** the problems in **minute** detail. A spokesperson said, 'It is an **insult** to suggest that staff are incompetent. The **content** of the report will show that we have had problems since the **contract** was placed with a new computer company.'

Listen and check. Practise reading the texts again.

7

Modal auxiliary verbs • *need* • Verbs related to modals • Phrasal verbs – type 4 • Consonant clusters • Sentence stress

Getting along

Revision of all modals

1 Meaning check

Tick (✓) the correct explanation for each of these modals.

1 Leanne may look for a new job.
- a ☐ Leanne has permission to look for a new job.
- b ☐ It's possible Leanne will look for a new job.

2 I couldn't swim until I was 16.
- a ☐ I wasn't allowed to swim until I was 16.
- b ☐ I wasn't able to swim until I was 16.

3 No one can smoke in pubs or restaurants.
- a ☐ No one is allowed to smoke in pubs or restaurants.
- b ☐ No one is able to smoke in pubs or restaurants.

4 You should wear glasses.
- a ☐ My advice is that you wear glasses.
- b ☐ It's possible that you will have to wear glasses.

5 Will you answer the phone?
- a ☐ I'm asking you to answer the phone.
- b ☐ Are you at some time in the future going to answer the phone?

6 I couldn't get the top off the jar.
- a ☐ I didn't manage to get the top off the jar.
- b ☐ I wasn't allowed to get the top off the jar.

7 You must be tired.
- a ☐ You are required to be tired.
- b ☐ I'm sure you are tired.

8 Andy's very busy, so he may not go to the party.
- a ☐ Andy doesn't have permission to go to the party.
- b ☐ There's a possibility Andy won't go to the party.

2 Which modal?

1 Complete the sentences with words from the box. Often there is more than one answer.

will	should	can	ought to	could
must	may	have to	might	

1 You __________ get your hair cut. It's too long.

2 __________ I ask you a question?

3 Young children __________ be carried on this escalator.

4 You __________ never get a seat on this train. It's always packed.

5 I __________ be studying Mandarin Chinese next year.

6 I __________ already speak five languages fluently.

7 You'll __________ work much harder if you want to pass.

8 It's Saturday night. There __________ be something good on TV.

9 You __________ leave your valuables in the hotel safe.

10 You __________ be over 1m 60cm tall to be a flight attendant.

2 Circle the correct answer.

1 You *mustn't* / *won't* have any problems with Josh. He's such a good baby.
2 You *don't have to* / *mustn't* use cream in this sauce, but it makes it much tastier.
3 I *couldn't* / *wouldn't* watch my favourite programme because Mia rang up for a long chat.
4 Timmy's so stubborn. He just *can't* / *won't* do what he's told.
5 I'm afraid I *can't* / *may not* come to your wedding as I'll be in Australia.
6 I *was able to* / *could* get 20% off the price in the sale.
7 You *don't have to* / *mustn't* say a word about this to your mother. It's a surprise.

3 Positive to negative

Rewrite the sentences to make them negative.

1 You must stop here.

____

2 We must learn the whole poem.

____

3 They had to take off their shoes.

____

4 He must be speaking Swedish.

____

5 They will have to wear a uniform at their new school.

____

6 You'll have to help me do this exercise.

____

4 Present probability

Respond to the statements or questions using the words in brackets. Put the verb in its correct form.

1 Harry is packing his suitcase. (must /go on holiday)

He must be going on holiday.

2 Jenny looks really unhappy. (must / miss / boyfriend)

____

3 Who's at the front door? (will / Tom)

____

4 Where's Kate? It's nearly lunchtime! (can't / still / sleep)

____

5 Why are all the lights on in their house? (could / have / party)

____

6 James has been working all night. (must / deadline to meet)

____

7 There's a thick fog this morning. (might / difficult / drive / work)

____

8 Timmy can't find his little sister. (may / hide / in the garden)

____

5 *need*

Need can work like a modal verb or a normal verb.

1 It is usually formed like a normal verb + infinitive with *to*.

*She **needs to go** to bed.*
*Does she **need to go** to bed?*
*She doesn't **need to go** to bed.*

2 *Need* is used as a modal verb mainly in the negative.

*She **needn't go** to bed yet.*

But it can sometimes be used as a question.

***Need I go** to bed?*

3 *Need* + *-ing* = *need* + passive infinitive.

*The car **needs fixing**.* = The car needs to be fixed.

1 Write **M** when *need* is used as a modal verb, and **F** when *need* is used as a full verb.

1 ☐ I need to go home.
2 ☐ You needn't come if you don't want to.
3 ☐ The business doesn't need to invest in more new technology.
4 ☐ Money is desperately needed to protect the world's endangered species.
5 ☐ Need I pay now, or can I pay later?
6 ☐ If you have any problems, you only need to tell us and we'll try to help.
7 ☐ The cooker needs cleaning.
8 ☐ Leave the washing-up. You needn't do it now.

2 Circle the correct verb. Sometimes two are correct.

1 I *mustn't / needn't / don't have to* do this exercise but it might help.
2 You *mustn't / needn't / don't have to* think I'm always this irritable. I've just had a bad day.
3 We *mustn't / needn't / don't have to* book a table. The restaurant won't be busy tonight.
4 Do you really *must / need to / have to* go now? Can't you stay a bit longer?
5 You *mustn't / don't need to / don't have to* eat all your vegetables. Just have the carrots.
6 Have I *must / need to / got to* ring and confirm my room reservation?
7 The carpet *needs / must / has to* replacing. Look at the state of it!

6 Modals review

Complete the conversations with a suitable modal verb and the correct form of the verbs in brackets.

1 **A** You really (1) __________ (go) to bed now, or you (2) __________ (feel) tired tomorrow.
B I'll go in a minute. I (3) __________ (finish) this revision first.
A You (4) __________ (pass) the exam easily. Get some rest now.

2 **A** It's five past eleven. Ken and Cathy's plane (5) __________ (touch down) in Kennedy Airport right now.
B Your watch (6) __________ (be) slow. It's nearly half past.
A It (7) __________ (be)! I've just had it repaired.

3 **A** Bring very warm clothes. It (8) __________ (snow) when we arrive.
B Oh, yes. I've heard it (9) __________ (snow) in the mountains even in summer.

4 **A** What are all those people doing with those lights and cameras?
B They (10) __________ (make) a film.
A Who's the leading man?
B Not sure. It (11) __________ (be) him over there. And do you think that she's the leading lady?
A She (12) __________ (be). She's certainly beautiful enough!

5 **A** What are you up to?
B Just doing the maths homework.
A Why are you doing that now? We (13) __________ (hand) it in for another week.
B Well, I (14) __________ (go) away at the weekend, so I want to get it out of the way now.

Vocabulary

7 Verbs related to modals

1 Read the problems and responses. Replace the words in *italics* with a modal verb, or an expression with a modal verb.

Ask Andrea YOUR PROBLEMS SOLVED ONLINE

Drowning in tech!

Dear Andrea,

I think there's something wrong with me. I know technology [1] *has the potential to* make life easier, but in my case it just makes me terribly anxious as I always feel there are so many things I [2] *need to* do. When someone texts, emails, or tweets me, I always think I [3] *need to* reply immediately, and I find it impossible to get anything done! I want to regain some control over my life, but at the moment, I [4] *don't* see a way out. I feel like I'm drowning in technology! Please help!

Joanna, Brighton

Joanna, there is nothing wrong with you. This is a problem we all face. Firstly, [5] *it is imperative that you* learn how to skim read effectively, then you [6] *will be able to* sift quickly through what is important and what isn't. In today's world, this is a skill we [7] *need to* develop, otherwise we [8] *are certain to* drown, and it's only going to get worse. Also, [9] *it is advisable to* prioritize your messages and remember there is no real need to respond immediately. Do you expect an immediate response when you text? I think not, and most of us don't.

Andrea

I must quit!

Dear Andrea,

[10] *It is essential that I* give up smoking. I [11] *am always able to* give up for a few days, but then something stressful happens, and I find myself reaching for the cigarettes. I've noticed that I [12] *am not able to* run for the bus without gasping for breath, and my girlfriend [13] *refuses to* kiss me if I've just been smoking. Please help, I'll try anything.

Graham, Manchester

Graham, you have real motivation to stop, which means you're halfway there. You've already managed without a cigarette for a few days, which shows that [14] *it is possible for you to* succeed. Recognize that you [15] *are going to* find it difficult, but that you [16] *don't* give in to temptation.

There are lots of therapies on the market that [17] *have the potential to* support you. The highest dosage nicotine patches have the lowest risk of relapse, but lozenges, gum, nasal spray, and inhalers are also available.

[18] *It is advisable that you* start on the higher dose and gradually reduce it to the lower levels. Avoid situations which you associate with smoking. You [19] *have the ability to* do this. Good luck!

Andrea

2 Rewrite the sentences using the prompts.

1 It's Anna's birthday tomorrow, so I should buy her a card. ('d better)

It's Anna's birthday tomorrow, so I'd better buy her a card.

2 Guests shouldn't leave valuables in their rooms. (advised)

____

3 You can't use your phone in the quiet carriage. (Using … permitted)

____

4 I'm sure he'll do well. He's so clever. (bound)

____

5 People under 18 shouldn't drink alcohol. (supposed)

____

6 You can't use dictionaries in this exam. (The use of dictionaries … allowed)

____

7 Travellers to the States need a visa. (required)

____

8 I expect you'll find it difficult to learn Russian. (likely)

____

9 I wasn't allowed to stay out late until I was 18. (parents … let)

____

Phrasal verbs

8 Type 4 – verb + adverb + preposition + object

1 Type 4 phrasal verbs have a verb + adverb + preposition. The preposition has an object.

*We've **run out of** sugar.*

Do you get on with your neighbours?

2 The word order cannot change.

*Do you **get on with** them?*

NOT ~~Do you get on them with?~~

*We've **run out of** it.*

NOT ~~We've run out it of.~~

3 Dictionaries show type 4 phrasal verbs by giving both the adverb and the preposition.

get away with sth: do something bad and not get punished for it

SWAG

4 Sometimes a phrasal verb can be type 4 or type 1.

Type 1: *Their marriage **broke up** last year.*

Type 4: *She's sad because she's just **broken up with** her boyfriend.*

Dictionaries show this.

break up (with sb)

▶▶ Type 1 see p22

Complete the sentences with the combinations in the box.

away with	off with	up for	up with	out of
on with (x 2)	out with (x2)	~~up to~~	down on	

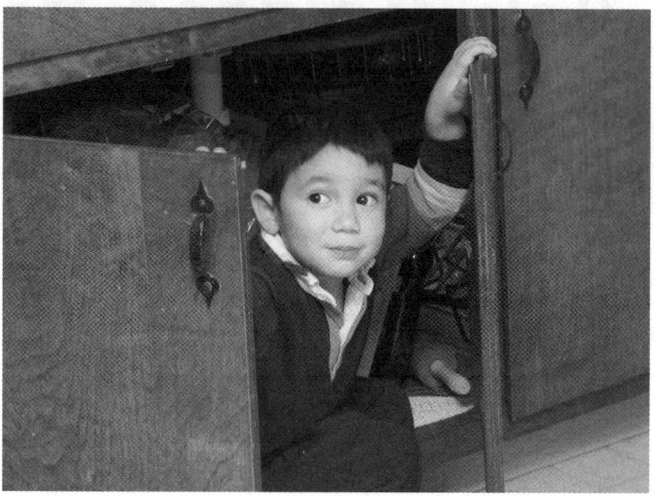

1 Joey! You've got a very guilty look on your face! What naughty things have you been getting ***up to*** this time?

2 The burglar broke into the house and made __________ a lot of jewellery.

3 We must try to cut __________ the amount of money we spend a month. We spend more than we earn.

4 Don't let me disturb you. Carry __________ your work.

5 I'm sorry we didn't get into the cinema. I'll take you to a restaurant to make __________ it. Does that cheer you up?

6 There is a move in Britain to do __________ the monarchy completely, so that Britain would become a republic.

7 Sam's mean with money, and he's always trying to get __________ paying his fair share of the bills for the flat.

8 I went __________ Aimee for two years, and then we broke up.

9 I can't put __________ Paul's rudeness a minute longer. I'm leaving him.

10 Judith is a very difficult person to get __________ . She's always falling __________ people.

Listening

9 Not getting on

1 Listen to the conversation and choose the best answer.

1 Sophie's upset about …
- a ☐ her friend.
- b ☐ the evening.
- c ☐ her boyfriend.

2 Charlie's …
- a ☐ ignored her.
- b ☐ been mean to her.
- c ☐ laughed at her.

3 Charlie's …
- a ☐ out of work.
- b ☐ having problems at work.
- c ☐ looking for a new job.

4 Anya wants Sophie to …
- a ☐ leave him.
- b ☐ be nice to him.
- c ☐ tell him to stop it.

5 Sophie …
- a ☐ agrees to this.
- b ☐ doesn't want to, because she loves him.
- c ☐ wants things to get magically better.

6 After talking to Anya, Sophie feels …
- a ☐ miserable.
- b ☐ more cheerful.
- c ☐ annoyed.

2 Listen again and complete these sentences.

Exaggeration and Understatement

1 You look ________________ ! ☐
2 I'm just ________________ , that's all. ☐
3 He made ________________ remarks this evening. ☐
4 He's been having ________________ at work recently. ☐
5 I think his behaviour is ________________ . ☐
6 It's getting me ________________ , I must say. ☐
7 I'm ________________ him, you know. ☐
8 You sound ________________ already! ☐

3 Which sentences from exercise 2 are examples of exaggeration (**E**) and which are understatement (**U**)?

Pronunciation

10 Consonant clusters

English has many words with groups (or clusters) of consonants:

happened	/hæpənd/
couldn't	/kʊdnt/
puzzles	/pʌzlz/

These words all have consonant clusters. Say them aloud and then transcribe them.

1	/'dʌznt/	______	7	/ædə'lesnt/	______
2	/'ʃʊdnt/	______	8	/ə'reɪndʒd/	______
3	/'mʌsnt/	______	9	/rɪ'leɪʃnʃɪp/	______
4	/'prɒmɪst/	______	10	/'æŋgri/	______
5	/ɒ'streɪlɪə/	______	11	/ɪk'saɪtmənt/	______
6	/plæŋks/	______	12	/ɪm'prest/	______

11 Sentence stress

Rob and Stuart are chatting about Frank. Read the conversation aloud and mark the stress in Stuart's responses.

1	**Rob**	Don't you think Frank's put on a lot of weight recently?
	Stuart	You're kidding. If anything, he's lost weight.
2	**Rob**	I think Frank earns more than me.
	Stuart	Well, I know he earns a lot more than me.
3	**Rob**	He's thinking of buying a second-hand Mercedes.
	Stuart	What do you mean? He's already bought a brand new one.
4	**Rob**	He's just bought two pairs of designer jeans.
	Stuart	Didn't you know that all Frank's clothes are designer labels?
5	**Rob**	Does Frank have many stocks and shares?
	Stuart	He has loads of them.
6	**Rob**	Isn't Frank in New York on business?
	Stuart	No, in fact he's in Florida on holiday.
7	**Rob**	His latest girlfriend has long, blonde hair.
	Stuart	Really? The girl I saw him with had short, brown hair.

8

Relative clauses • Participles
• Adjectives • Nouns in groups • Adjectives and prepositions
• Silent consonants

How remarkable!

Defining and non-defining relative clauses

1 General knowledge quiz

Test your general knowledge. Tick (✔) the correct answer.

Remarkable things, people, and places

1 **The first video that reached one billion views on YouTube was**
  a ☐ the wedding of Prince William and Kate Middleton.
  b ☐ the Korean pop song 'Gangnam Style'.
  c ☐ Barack Obama's 2012 victory speech.

2 **The first woman**
  a ☐ who walked to the North Pole
  b ☐ who skied to the South Pole
  c ☐ who climbed Everest
  was Felicity Aston.

3 **A megacity is a city which has more than**
  a ☐ 10 million inhabitants.
  b ☐ 15 million inhabitants.
  c ☐ 20 million inhabitants.

4 **The Statue of Liberty, which was a gift from France to the USA,**
  a ☐ is the tallest statue in the world.
  b ☐ is the heaviest statue in the world.
  c ☐ is made from bronze.

5 **The most expensive hotel in the world, where a suite costs $81,000 a night,**
  a ☐ is Burj Al Arab, in Dubai.
  b ☐ is The Raj Palace Hotel, in Jaipur.
  c ☐ is Hotel President Wilson, in Geneva.

6 **Lewis Carroll,**
  a ☐ whose real name was Charles Lutwidge Dodgson,
  b ☐ whose real name was Clive Staples Lewis,
  c ☐ whose real name was Christopher James Dalton,
  wrote several famous poems and books, including *Alice in Wonderland*.

7 **Central Park, which is in New York City,**
  a ☐ is the most filmed location in the world.
  b ☐ is the largest urban park in the world.
  c ☐ is the smallest urban park in the world.

8 **The largest hot desert on Earth is the Sahara,**
  a ☐ which is 14 million square kilometres.
  b ☐ which is 4 million square kilometres.
  c ☐ which is 10 million square kilometres.

2 Defining or non-defining?

1 Decide if these sentences are best completed with a defining relative clause (D) or a non-defining relative clause (ND). Write **D** or **ND** in the boxes.

1 [ ] I'd love to meet someone ________________ .
2 [ ] We're looking for a house ________________ .
3 [ ] We went to see *Romeo and Juliet* ________________ .
4 [ ] Do you know a shop ________________ ?
5 [ ] Marilyn Monroe ________________ died of a drug overdose.
6 [ ] I find people ________________ difficult to get on with.
7 [ ] My computer ________________ is already out of date.
8 [ ] I met a girl ________________ .
9 [ ] Professor Brian Cox ________________ will give a talk next week.
10 [ ] I bought a cheese and pickle sandwich ________________ .

2 Complete the sentences in exercise 1 with this information. Add a relative pronoun and commas where necessary. Leave out the relative pronoun if possible.

You went to school with her.
I ate it immediately.
It has four bedrooms.
I bought it only last year.
They lose their temper easily.
It sells second-hand furniture.
Her real name was Norma Jean Baker.
This person could teach me how to cook.
He's a well-known physicist and TV presenter.
I really enjoyed it.

3 Punctuation and omitting the pronoun

Add commas to these sentences if they have a non-defining relative clause. If possible, cross out the pronoun in the defining relative clauses.

1 Sheila, who I first got to know at university, was one of six children.
2 The man ~~who~~ you were talking to is a famous artist.
3 This is the story that amazed the world. (no change)
4 The thing that I most regret is not going to university.
5 My two daughters who are 16 and 13 are both interested in dancing.
6 The town where I was born has changed dramatically.
7 I didn't like the clothes which were in the sale.
8 The phone that I bought yesterday doesn't work.
9 The part of Europe where I'd most like to live is Portugal.
10 The Algarve where my mother's family comes from is famous for its beautiful beaches and dramatic coastline.
11 Salt that comes from the sea is considered to be the best for cooking.
12 Salt whose qualities have been known since prehistoric times is used to season and preserve food.

4 All relative pronouns

1 Match a line in **A** with a line in **B**.

A	B
1 Have I told you recently	a ☐ when you expect to arrive.
2 I have to do	b ☐ where my brother lives.
3 We were stuck in traffic for hours,	c ☐ which came as a bit of a surprise.
4 We're emigrating to Australia,	d ☐ whose body was covered in tattoos.
5 I met a girl	e [1] how much I love you?
6 I passed all my exams,	f ☐ whatever you want.
7 Let me know	g ☐ which was a nightmare.
8 I'll buy you	h ☐ what I believe to be right.

2 Complete the sentences with a relative pronoun. If the pronoun can be omitted, add nothing.

1 The lady __________ is sitting in the wheelchair is my grandmother.
2 I know an Italian restaurant __________ serves excellent pasta.
3 I know an Italian restaurant __________ you can always get a table.
4 Uncle Tom earns a fortune, __________ is why I've asked him to lend me £1,000.
5 Sean is a child __________ people immediately like.
6 My daughter, __________ ambition is to emigrate to Australia, has finally got her visa.
7 I gave him a glass of water, __________ he drank thirstily.
8 The flight __________ we wanted to get was fully booked.
9 My auntie's house is the place __________ I feel most at home.
10 This is the smallest car __________ has ever been made.
11 That's the man __________ wife left him because he kept his pet snake in their bedroom.
12 I love the things __________ you say to me.
13 I go shopping at the new shopping centre, __________ there's always free parking.
14 She told me she'd been married before, __________ I hadn't realized.
15 __________ you do, don't touch that button. It turns off the power.

5 Prepositions in relative clauses

Combine the sentences, keeping the preposition after the verb in the relative clause.

1 I want you to meet the people. I work with them.
I want you to meet the people I work with.

2 She's a friend. I can always rely on her.
____
____

3 That's the man. The police were looking for him.
____
____

4 She recommended a book by Robert Palmer. I'd never heard of him.
____
____

5 You paid £200 for a pair of trainers. They have been reduced to £100.
The trainers __________
____

6 This is the book. I was telling you about it.
____
____

7 The Prime Minister gave a good speech. I agree with his views.
____
____

8 His talk was on the environment. I care deeply about this.
____
____

9 What's that music? You're listening to it.
____
____

10 My mother died last week. I looked after her for many years.
____
____

Participles

6 Participles as adjectives

Complete the adjectives with -ed or -ing.

1 a shock_ing_ fact
2 a reserv_ed_ seat
3 scream_____ babies
4 a satisfi_____ customer
5 a disgust_____ meal
6 a confus_____ explanation
7 a challeng_____ job
8 a conceit_____ person
9 a frighten_____ film
10 an exhaust_____ walk
11 a disappoint_____ outcome
12 a tir_____ journey
13 an unexpect_____ visit
14 disturb_____ images
15 a thrill_____ story
16 an amus_____ remark
17 a disappoint_____ customer
18 well-behav_____ children
19 a promis_____ start
20 a cake load_____ with calories

7 Participle clauses

1 Rewrite the sentences with a present or past participle clause instead of a relative clause.

1 Can you see the woman who's dressed in red over there?
Can you see the woman dressed in red over there?

2 People who live in blocks of flats often complain of loneliness.
____

3 Letters that are posted before 5.00 p.m. should arrive the next day.
____

4 The train that is standing on platform five is for Manchester.
____

5 Firemen have rescued passengers who were trapped in the accident.
____

6 They live in a lovely house that overlooks the River Thames.
____

7 It took workmen days to clear up the litter that was dropped by the crowds.
____

2 Complete the sentences with a verb from the box in either its present or past participle form.

feel	borrow	explain	say	~~ruin~~	study	take	pass	steal

1 My dad was in a bad mood for the whole week, completely _ruining_ the holiday.
2 After __________ all her exams with A grades, Maggie went out to celebrate.
3 Jewellery __________ in the robbery has never been recovered.
4 I got a letter from the Tax Office __________ that I owe them £1,000.
5 __________ hungry, I decided to make myself a sandwich.
6 Books __________ from the library must be returned in two weeks.
7 I had a long talk to Ruby, __________ why it was important for her to work hard.
8 __________ everything into consideration, I've decided to give you a second chance.
9 With both children __________ at university, the house seems really quiet.

Relatives and participles review

8 Fearless Felix

Read and complete the article with the clauses in the box.

Relative clause
which has put him
that scared him
who jumped
what no man has done
whose skydiving career
from which he would leap
which can happen when
whose fear of being enclosed
Past participle
known as Fearless Felix
terrified of wearing
Present participle
including his mother and his girlfriend
knowing he had to

THE 24-MILE JUMP FROM SPACE

Felix Baumgartner, otherwise [1] ___________, is the Austrian man [2] ___________ from the edge of space and became the first man to break the speed of sound in free fall.

Baumgartner, [3] ___________ spanned nearly two decades before he started training for his most daring skydive of all, was, understandably, afraid of the challenge. However, it wasn't the magnitude of the dive [4] ___________ most, but rather the outfit he had to wear to travel through space.

The skydiver, [5] ___________ was, incredibly, greater than his fear of doing the jump itself, had problems with the pressurized space suit. [6] ___________ a suit that restricted his movement, and [7] ___________ overcome his fear, Felix sought psychiatric help from a sports psychologist.

When he finally stood high above the Earth in the helium balloon, [8] ___________ into space, he looked a solitary and vulnerable figure. There was every chance he could be falling into oblivion. At last, Felix jumped and immediately started to spin out of control, [9] ___________ you travel at such a high speed. His 100-strong support team, [10] ___________, watched with their hearts in their mouths. However, Felix managed to stabilize himself and fulfill his dream. Baumgartner has done [11] ___________ before: he has plummeted through 24 miles of cold, dark space at a speed of 843.6 miles per hour, a feat [12] ___________ in *The Guinness Book of Records.*

Vocabulary

9 People, places, and things

1 Complete the table with these descriptive adjectives. There are six in each group.

~~unspoilt~~	stubborn	breathtaking	cracked	arrogant
humble	picturesque	automatic	conceited	handmade
loyal	waterproof	desolate	priceless	considerate
overcrowded	smashed	built-up		

People	Places	Things
	unspoilt	

2 Complete the sentences with an adjective from exercise 1.

1 The view from the top of the mountain was absolutely __________ .
2 He's always boasting about how great he is at everything. He's so __________ .
3 Our new car is fully __________ . I don't want to change gears when I'm driving any more.
4 He is so kind and __________; he's always going out of his way to help people.
5 The countryside was completely __________ – rolling hills and green fields for miles around.
6 The Cotswolds is an area in England which is very __________ . It has lots of pretty, old-fashioned villages.
7 He's really __________ . He won't do a thing they tell him.
8 That bag you're looking at is __________ by local craftsmen. Look at the quality of the work.
9 The beach was seriously __________ . There was no room to put our towels down.

10 Nouns in groups

Look at these examples of number + noun + noun.

a three-mile walk
a 16-year-old girl
a ten-hour flight

These are expressions of measurement before a noun.
The number and the first noun are joined with a hyphen, and the first noun is usually in the singular.

Put the information before the noun.

1 a note that is worth ten pounds
____
2 a language course that lasts eight weeks
____
3 a drive that takes six hours
____
4 a meal that consists of three courses
____
5 a holiday that lasts one month
____
6 a delay at the airport that went on for four hours
____
7 a document that has 100 pages
____
8 a university course that takes three years
____
9 a prison sentence of ten years
____
10 a hotel with five stars
____
11 a speed limit of 30 mph
____
12 a house that is 200 years old
____

Prepositions

11 Adjective + preposition

Complete these sentences with the correct preposition.

1 Are you afraid ______ the dark?
2 She was angry ______ me ______ not telling her the news.
3 Canterbury is famous ______ its cathedral.
4 Bill is jealous ______ me because I'm so much cleverer than him.
5 I'm very proud ______ my two daughters.
6 I'm disappointed ______ you. I thought I could trust you.
7 You're very different ______ your brother. I thought you'd be similar ______ each other.
8 Are you excited ______ going on holiday?
9 Visitors to Britain aren't used ______ driving on the left.
10 Visitors to hot countries need to be aware ______ the risk of malaria.
11 You should be ashamed ______ what you did.
12 I am most grateful ______ all your help.
13 Who is responsible ______ this mess?
14 What's wrong ______ you? You don't look well.
15 My son is crazy ______ a band called *Moones*.

Pronunciation

12 Silent consonants

1 English words often have silent consonants:

know writer walk climb

Complete the table with these words. Cross out the silent consonants.

~~industry~~	honest	executive	inhabitant
~~receipt~~	distinctly	rebuilt	fasten
eccentric	insect	lamp	sumptuous
exhausted	whistle	straight	anonymous
citizen	fascinating	delighted	documentary
landscape	temperature	business	debt

Silent consonants	No silent consonants
receipt	*industry*

2 Write these words. They all have silent consonants.

1 /saɪn/ ______
2 /saɪˈkaɪətrɪst/ ______
3 /ˈhænsəm/ ______
4 /ˈaɪlənd/ ______
5 /ˈkrɪsməs/ ______
6 /ˈfraɪtnd/ ______
7 /ˈklaɪmə/ ______
8 /ˈgrænfɑːðə/ ______
9 /ˈnɒlɪdʒ/ ______
10 /kɑːm/ ______

Expressing habit • *get* and *be* • Homonyms and homophones • Phrasal verbs and nouns that go together • Weak and strong forms

The way we were

Present and past habit

1 Present habit

Match a sentence in **A** with a sentence in **B**.

A	B
1 She's really generous.	a ☐ She **jogs** to work every day.
2 He's so disorganized.	b ☐ They **get** everything they ask for.
3 She's very fashionable.	c ☐ She **never thinks** before she speaks.
4 He's so dishonest.	d ☐ He **never plans** anything properly.
5 She's so sensitive.	e ☐ He**'s always applying** for new jobs.
6 He's really stubborn.	f ☐ He**'s always telling** lies.
7 She's so rude.	g ☐ She**'s always buying** me presents.
8 They're so spoilt.	h ☐ She**'ll** only **wear** designer clothes.
9 She's very energetic.	i ☐ She**'ll start** crying at the slightest thing.
10 He's very ambitious.	j ☐ He **won't** ever **change** his mind.

2 My family's bad habits

Rewrite the sentences in one or two ways using *will/won't* and/or the Present Continuous.

1 My dad mends his motorbike in the living room.

a ______________________________

b ______________________________

2 My brother leaves the top off the toothpaste.

a ______________________________

b ______________________________

3 He doesn't help with the household chores.

a ______________________________

4 My sister borrows my clothes without asking.

a ______________________________

b ______________________________

5 My grandpa doesn't let anyone choose what's on TV.

a ______________________________

6 My grandma gossips about the neighbours.

a ______________________________

b ______________________________

7 Carole and Alan boast about their children.

a ______________________________

b ______________________________

3 Past habit – *used to*

Complete the sentences with the correct form of *used to*: positive, question, or negative.

1 My grandfather never __________ get so out of breath when he climbed the stairs.
2 There __________ be a beautiful old building where that car park is now.
3 __________ have a Saturday job when you were at school?
4 She __________ be so moody. It's only since she lost her job.
5 __________ play cricket when you were at school?
6 Julie __________ be as slim as she is now. She's been dieting.
7 Where __________ go out to eat when you lived in Madrid?
8 __________ smoke 60 cigarettes a day? How did you give up?

4 It's so annoying!

Tick (✔) the sentences where the speaker is annoyed by someone's behaviour.

1 ☐ He watches sports programmes on TV.
☐ He's always watching sports programmes on TV.

2 ☐ She'd give us extra lessons after school.
☐ She *would* give us extra lessons after school.
☐ She was always giving us homework.
☐ She used to give us homework.

3 ☐ Our cat always used to sleep on my bed.
☐ Our cat would always sleep on *my* bed.
☐ Our cat always slept on my bed.

4 ☐ My boss is always asking me to stay late.
☐ My boss often asks me to stay late.

5 ☐ My children don't help out at home.
☐ My children will never help out at home.

5 *used to* and *would*

Which of the verb forms can complete the sentences below? Tick (✔) all possible answers.

1 I _____ long blonde hair when I was first married.
a ☑ had b ☑ used to have c ☐ would have

2 We _____ every summer with our cousins in Scotland.
a ☐ spent b ☐ used to spend c ☐ would spend

3 Pam _____ out with Andy for six months but then she ditched him.
a ☐ went b ☐ used to go c ☐ would go

4 We _____ coffee and croissants every morning for breakfast.
a ☐ had b ☐ used to have c ☐ would have

5 We _____ to each other every day when we were apart.
a ☐ wrote b ☐ used to write c ☐ would write

6 He _____ to me for 20 years and then stopped.
a ☐ wrote b ☐ used to write c ☐ would write

7 In the old days, people _____ you if you were in trouble.
a ☐ helped b ☐ used to help c ☐ would help

8 I _____ living so close to the sea.
a ☐ loved b ☐ used to love c ☐ would love

9 Dave _____ Molly three times if she wanted to go out with him.
a ☐ asked b ☐ used to ask c ☐ would ask

10 I _____ questions in class. I was too shy.
a ☐ never asked b ☐ never used to ask
c ☐ would never ask

11 Before I worked here, I _____ as an assistant manager at a restaurant.
a ☐ worked b ☐ used to work c ☐ would work

12 When I was a child, I _____ hours helping my mother in the garden.
a ☐ often spent b ☐ often used to spend
c ☐ would often spend

6 *get* and *be*

1 *Get used to* means *become used to* and describes a change of state. *Be used to* describes a state. Compare these sentences.

Don't worry. You'll soon ***get used to*** *working such long hours.*

I'm used to *working long hours. I've done it for years.*

He eventually ***got used to*** *the tropical climate, but it took a long time.*

*He was born in India, so he****'s used to*** *a hot climate.*

2 *Get* + adjective usually means *become*.

The sea's ***getting rough****. Let's go back!*

3 *Get* + past participle can be used to describe things we do to ourselves. It can also be used to describe things that happen to us, often negative events. Compare these sentences.

I ***got dressed*** *and went to work.*

We ***got married*** *last week.*

I ***got lost*** *on the mountain.*

4 *Get* + infinitive can mean *have the opportunity to do something*. It can also describe a gradual change. Compare these sentences.

She'll be furious if she ***gets to hear*** *about this.*

As I ***got to know*** *Paris, I started to like it more and more.*

1 Complete the sentences with *used to*, *be used to*, or *get used to* in the correct form, positive or negative.

1 If you __________ Indian food, this dish might be too spicy for you.

2 I'll never __________ your hair that short. You'll have to grow it again.

3 **A** How do you drive in all this traffic?
B I __________ it now, so it's OK. But it took me a while to __________ it, believe me!

4 Tom didn't like his new school at first, but he eventually __________ it, and made new friends.

5 I __________ jog every morning, but I don't any more. I'm so unfit now.

6 When I was a boy, I __________ like going to piano lessons, so I stopped. Now I'm in my forties, I've started learning again!

7 Sally won't find it easy to live on her own. She __________ her parents doing everything for her.

8 **A** I hate my new job!
B Give it a chance. You may __________ it after you've been there a bit longer.

9 'Grandad, __________ you really __________ watch TV in black and white when you were young?'

10 **A** __________ you __________ your new teacher yet? I know you didn't like her much at first.
B Well, I have a bit. She's OK, I suppose.

2 Complete the sentences with *get* or *be* in the correct form and a word or expression from the box.

better	ready (x 2)	dressed	dark	engaged
to know	a pilot	lost	upset	

1 I often __________ when I watch the news. Such awful things are happening in the world.

2 **A** How are you feeling?
B I __________ slowly, but I still feel weak.

3 My little nephew is determined __________ when he grows up.

4 **A** Come on, Helen! The play starts in half an hour.
B I __________ in two minutes. I __________ just __________ and putting my shoes on.
A I don't know why it takes you so long. I __________ since 6.00.

5 **A** Do we turn right or left at the next junction?
B I've no idea! I think we __________ .

6 **A** Did you hear that Sue and Chris __________ ?
B No! I never thought they would!

7 I didn't use to like Mick at all, but the more I __________ him, the more I like him. Now he's my best friend!

8 In summer, it is still light at 9.00 in the evening, but in winter, it __________ at 5.00.

7 The day we met

1 Read the story. Which of the verbs in italics … ?

a … can change to both *used to* or *would*

b … can change only to *used to*

c … must stay in the Past Simple

Write **a**, **b**, or **c** next to the verbs

Punk love

by Serena Fraser

It was the summer of '76. I was 15, and I was sunbathing in a local park when I [1] c *looked* up and saw the strangest-looking person. I [2] ______ *wore* flared trousers, mini-skirts, and flowery shirts like most teenagers, but this guy [3] ______ *looked* like he'd just landed from another planet. He [4] ______ *had* a spiky, blue Mohican, and despite the heat, he [5] ______ *was* dressed from head to toe in black leather! I was fascinated, so I [6] ______ *went* to the park regularly just to catch a glimpse of him. He and his friends [7] ______ *hung out* there most days. They [8] ______ *wore* a lot of make-up, even the boys, and their hair [9] ______ *changed* colour all the time! One day, he [10] ______ *spotted* me and [11] ______ *beckoned* me over. He [12] ______ *looked* so scary with his now green hair and black make-up, but I really wanted to meet him, so I [13] ______ *walked* over to say 'Hi'.

His name was Alan, he was 17, and he [14] ______ *studied* art at the local college. Even though he [15] ______ *dressed* weirdly, he was really interesting. I [16] ______ *spent* all my free time with him after that. We [17] ______ *met* in the park, or at the Bel café if we [18] ______ *had* any money, and we [19] ______ *talked* about art, music, politics, and all kinds of things. I [20] ______ *started* to dress like him and his friends, and Alan [21] ______ *came* with me when I got my first Mohican and [22] ______ *became* a proper punk! He [23] ______ *took* me to see lots of great punk bands like The Clash and the Sex Pistols. Alan [24] ______ *sang* in a band called Social Misfits, and he [25] ______ *pranced* about on stage like a mad thing. We [26] ______ *loved* going to gigs all over London.

We [27] ______ *got married* in 1980, dressed in black leather. Our three children [28] ______ *giggled* over our wedding photos, never quite believing that their parents [29] ______ *were* punks. We're quite normal-looking nowadays, but we still wear our black leather jackets to remind ourselves we weren't always middle-aged!

2 Complete these sentences about the story with one suitable word from the box.

got used wasn't would

1 Serena often ____________ to go to the park.

2 She ____________ go just to see the weird-looking guy.

3 He and his friends ____________ to wear a lot of make-up and dye their hair.

4 Serena ____________ used to seeing men wearing make-up. She thought it strange.

5 However, she soon ____________ used to the way they looked.

6 She ____________ to know Alan very well.

7 She ____________ to meet him regularly, and they ____________ go for a coffee.

8 She got ____________ to listening to punk music. She ____________ to like it.

Vocabulary

8 Homonyms

Use the same word to complete each pair of sentences.

1 **a** The sun rose brightly over the house this morning.
  b He's very romantic. He always gives me a red rose when we go on a date.

2 **a** Look out of the window, Josie – there's Daddy coming up the path! ___________ to him!
  b With each huge ___________, the ferry rocked, and I began to feel really sick.

3 **a** Look, I've no idea what you're arguing about. What ___________ are you trying to make?
  b He couldn't speak the language, so he just used to ___________ whenever he wanted something.

4 **a** Everyone has the ___________ to a fair trial.
  b Well done! You got all the answers ___________ in the test.

5 **a** Gosh, you look smart! Is that a new ___________ and tie you're wearing?
  b Well, I think you should buy the pale green dress. The red one doesn't ___________ you.

6 **a** See the man with blue eyes and ___________ hair? That's Jenny's husband.
  b It's not ___________! You gave him more than me!

7 **a** Oh, look! Justin Bieber's on at the Palladium. Can we get tickets? I'm a real ___________ of his.
  b It's boiling hot. Could we switch the ___________ on and get some air circulating?

8 **a** He noticed the thin gold ___________ on her ring finger.
  b He used to play in a rock ___________ in his youth.

9 Homophones

Write the correct spelling of the words in phonetics.

Phonetic symbols p100

1 **a** I'm /bɔːd/! I can't think of anything to do.
  b He jumped on his surf /bɔːd/ and paddled out to the biggest waves.

  a ___________ b ___________

2 **a** Stop it! You know you aren't /əlaʊd/ to do that!
  b Michael, please stand up and read your story /əlaʊd/ to the class.

  a ___________ b ___________

3 **a** She was happy to get her bag back when the police /kɔːt/ the thief.
  b The thief was sentenced to three months in prison at /kɔːt/ the next day.

  a ___________ b ___________

4 **a** Sara took out a /ləʊn/ to pay for her university course.
  b The bad weather prevented us from climbing any further, but we could see one /ləʊn/ climber on the summit.

  a ___________ b ___________

5 **a** We looked for a car /haɪə/ place in our holiday resort so that we could travel around a bit.
  b Throw the ball /haɪə/ or you'll never get it in the basket!

  a ___________ b ___________

Q What sort of crisps can fly?

A Plain crisps.

Patient Doctor, I keep thinking I'm a billiard ball.

Doctor Go to the end of the cue.

Phrasal verbs

10 Phrasal verbs and nouns that go together

1 Some phrasal verbs have a strong association with certain objects: *set out on a journey; work out the solution to a problem.*

Match a verb with an object. There may be more than one answer, but there is one that is best.

1	come up with	a	☐	someone you respect
2	break into	b	☐	a naughty child
3	break off	c	☐	a problem, a complaint, a difficult customer
4	tell off	d	☐	the other people in the group
5	bring up	e	☐	a university course after one year
6	count on	f	☐	a solution to a problem
7	deal with	g	☐	your best friend to help you
8	drop out of	h	☐	children to be honest and hard-working
9	fit in with	i	☐	a house or a flat, to steal something
10	look up to	j	☐	a fact that someone might not be aware of
11	point out	k	☐	what I said – I didn't mean it
12	take back	l	☐	a relationship, an engagement

2 Complete the sentences with the correct form of a phrasal verb from exercise 1.

1 The thieves ___________ the warehouse and stole goods worth £20,000.
2 He ___________ his elder sister because she always seemed so wise and experienced.
3 I accused you of being mean the other day. I ___________ it all ___________ . I'm sorry.
4 I hadn't noticed that the living room was a different colour until someone ___________ it ___________ to me.
5 Scientists will have to ___________ new methods of increasing the world's food supply.
6 She ___________ Tom ___________ because he hit his sister.
7 You have a problem with your order, madam? I'll just get someone to ___________ it for you.
8 I had a new student today. He seems very nice. I'm sure he'll ___________ the rest of the class just fine.
9 Why did you ___________ university after just one term? What are you going to do now?
10 I'm running for President. I hope I can ___________ your support.
11 My parents ___________ me ___________ to finish all the food on my plate.
12 It was never going to work, so Marie and Jim decided to ___________ their engagement.

Listening

11 A small disagreement

1 🎧 Listen to the conversation between a young couple, Megan and Harry. Mark these statements true (✔) or false (✗). Correct the false ones.

1 They are arguing about a film they have seen. ☐
2 They would both often watch TV talent shows when they were at university. ☐
3 These programmes always used to make them cry. ☐
4 Megan believes that the format of these shows has become too predictable. ☐
5 Last year's winner was a girl called Ella with an amazing voice. ☐
6 Harry takes these shows very seriously. ☐
7 Megan thinks it's time Harry acted his age. ☐
8 Megan persuades Harry to watch a film with her. ☐

2 🎧 Look at the phrases in bold that Megan and Harry use to make their points. Listen again and complete the lines from their conversation.

1 **If you want my opinion**, it's ___________, over the top, and ___________ predictable.
2 **The problem now is that** it's the same ___________ format.
3 **I don't agree that** it's a ___________ .
4 **The point I'm trying to make** is that most of them ___________ !
5 **If you ask me**, you're ___________ off watching a good film.
6 **To tell you the truth**, I don't mind being ___________ .
7 **I know what you say is true**, but I ___________ .
8 **The main point** is not to take it too ___________ , which you ___________ do.

Pronunciation

12 Weak and strong forms

Auxiliary verbs have weak and strong forms, depending on whether they are unstressed or stressed.

1 Sometimes the weak form is a contraction.

he is = he's

she does not = she doesn't

I have not = I haven't

2 Sometimes the weak form is a change in the vowel sound. This is often a change to /ə/.

	Weak	Strong
was	/wəz/ *Was Tom there?*	/wɒz/ *Yes, he was.*
were	/wə/ *Were you there?*	/wɜː/ *Yes, we were.*
can	/kən/ *Can you swim?*	/kæn/ (can't = /kɑːnt/) *Yes, I can.*
been	/bɪn/ *I've been shopping*	/biːn/ *Where have you been?*

Some prepositions also have weak and strong vowel sounds.

	Weak	Strong		Weak	Strong
to	/tə/	/tuː/	for	/fə/	/fɔː/
of	/əv/	/ɒv/	from	/frəm/	/frɒm/
at	/ət/	/æt/			

1 Listen and (circle) all the weak vowel sounds in the sentences. Underline all those with strong vowels

1 I (don't) want (to) see him but (I)'m sure you want to.
2 Sue isn't going to learn from the experience, but Tom is.
3 I've heard that you're thinking of moving from London. Are you?
4 They have dinner at seven, don't they?
5 You'll be able to get a ticket for me, won't you?
6 I've got no idea who this letter's from.
7 Can't you remember who Bill used to work for?
8 I've been waiting for you to come. Where were you?
9 We'd been looking forward to coming for ages, then at the last minute we weren't able to.
10 Won't you sit down for a couple of minutes?

2 Read the telephone conversation between two friends and transcribe **A**'s lines. Add punctuation to make the meaning clear.

▶▶ **Phonetic symbols p100**

A /wɒt ə jə duːɪŋ ət ðə wiːkend/ ?

What are you doing at the weekend?

B I haven't decided yet.

A /wɪə gəʊɪŋ tə skɒtlənd djə wɒntə kʌm tuː/ ?

____

____

B I'd love to. Where are you staying?

A /wiv dɪsaɪdɪd tə kæmp nʌn əv ʌs kən əfɔːd tə peɪ fər ə həʊtel/

____

____

B Camping in Scotland in October! You'll be freezing cold.

A /nəʊ wi wəʊnt wiv gɒt strɒŋ tents lɒts əv wɔːm kləʊz ən θɪk sliːpɪŋ bægz/

____

____

B Have you checked the weather forecast?

A /əv kɔːs wi hæv ən ɪts prɪti wɔːm fər ɒktəʊbə/

____

____

B OK then. It'll be quite an adventure!

A /eksələnt aɪl tel ðɪ ʌðəz ðeɪl bi dɪlaɪtəd wiːl pɪk juː ʌp ət sɪks ɒn fraɪdeɪ siː juː ðen gʊdbaɪ/

____

____

B Bye!

Listen and check.

10

Modal auxiliary verbs in the past • Body idioms
• Verbs + prepositions • Rhymes and limericks

Over my dead body!

Revision of modals

1 Present to past

Rewrite the sentences to make them refer to the past.

1 I must read *Richard III* before my course begins.

I had to read Richard III before my course began.

2 I have to take the pills three times a day.

____

____

3 They must be away on holiday.

____

4 We can't have a lunch break – there's too much to do!

____

____

5 He can't be a millionaire.

____

6 We mustn't shout in the classroom.

____

____

7 He won't go to bed.

____

8 That will be John on the phone.

____

9 You should be more careful.

____

10 You could help with the washing-up for a change.

____

____

Modal verbs of probability

2 How certain?

1 Decide on the degree of certainty in these sentences. Put two ticks (✔✔) if the idea expressed is certain. Put one tick (✔) if it is less certain.

1 [✔✔] You must have seen him at the cinema. I know he was there.
2 [✔] The dog is really dirty. He might have been swimming in the lake.
3 [ ] He can't have been telling the truth.
4 [ ] He might have left a message on your mobile.
5 [ ] I don't know where she is. She may have gone shopping.
6 [ ] She must have been very upset when you told her the news.
7 [ ] They're not answering their phone. They must have gone away already.
8 [ ] I don't see their car. They can't have come back yet.
9 [ ] It's six o'clock. Tom will have gone home by now.
10 [ ] Matthew isn't here – he might have thought you weren't coming and gone to the cinema by himself.
11 [ ] I could have cancelled the meeting if I'd known earlier!
12 [ ] Ian will be back soon. It's Friday. He'll have gone to the pub after work.

Listen and notice the stress and intonation.

2 Make sentences from the table.

If I go to Norway, I If I went to Norway, I If I'd gone to Norway, I	can will may might would could	see the fjords. have seen the fjords.

1 _______________
2 _______________
3 _______________
4 _______________
5 _______________
6 _______________

3 Past probability

1 Write sentences for the situations below, using the information in the box.

He She They	must have can't have might have	cut it gone mislaid arrived home got engaged had been doing been making	a cake. a party last night. to Andy. something naughty. for ages. without me. by now. my number.

1 Stella's wearing a beautiful diamond ring.

____

____

2 The children ran away laughing and giggling.

____

____

3 There's flour on grandma's nose.

____

____

4 Paulo and Geri said they'd wait for me, but I can't see them.

____

____

5 Tim's flat is so clean and tidy.

____

____

6 It's after midnight. Henri and Sally left ages ago.

____

____

7 I don't know why Tara didn't ring.

____

____

8 Look at Joe's hair. It's really long!

____

____

2 Write sentences for the situations below using the information in the box in the perfect infinitive passive.

It They	must have been can't have been	washed hit blown down repaired dry-cleaned	by the wind. by a stone. properly. recently. with something red.

1 A tree has fallen across the road.

____

____

2 My white jeans have turned pink!

____

____

3 My TV has broken and I've only just had it fixed.

____

____

4 David's suit looks a bit dirty.

____

____

5 The car windscreen has shattered.

____

____

Ruby must have eaten it.

4 Past modals of deduction

Complete the conversations with the correct form of the verbs in brackets.

1 **A** I wonder how the thief got into our apartment?
B He [1] __________ (could / use) the fire escape or he [2] __________ (might / climb up) that tree.
A Well, he [3] __________ (need not / bother). There's nothing to steal!

2 **A** Bill told me that he'd spent £2,000 on a birthday present for his girlfriend, but he [4] __________ (must / joke). Surely he [5] __________ (can not / spend) that much.
B I think you [6] __________ (might / mishear) him!

3 **A** It's 3.30. Mum and Dad's plane landed over an hour ago. They [7] __________ (should / phone)!
B They [8] __________ (may / be delayed). No, look! They're driving up now. You [9] __________ (need not / worry).

4 **A** You're very sunburnt. You [10] __________ (would not / burn) if you'd used your factor 30 suncream.
B I [11] __________ (must / fall) asleep. And I [12] __________ (can not / put on) enough cream. Ouch!

5 Past modals – revision of all modal verbs

Circle the correct answer.

1 I'm sorry. I *shouldn't have / couldn't have* told Tom what you said about him.

2 **A** Where's the dog?
B Don't know. Dad *may have / 'll have* taken him for a walk.
A No. I remember. It's Tuesday, isn't it? Mum *should have / 'll have* taken him to the vet.

3 **A** Are Pat and Jan definitely coming? I*'d have / might have* thought they'd have arrived by now.
B They *should have / could have* been held up by traffic, don't you think?
A Or they *might have / needn't have* had an accident!
B Don't be silly. Anyway, we*'d have / must have* heard by now if something like that had happened.
A Well, I *needn't have / mustn't have* prepared lunch so early. And I think they *should have / may have* rung if they knew they were going to be late.

4 **A** Who was that man?
B He *can't have / must have* been a friend of Jane's. He was asking if I'd seen her.

Conman Canoe man

John Darwin claimed it [1] could not have been (can not/be) easier to fake his own death and get away with it, but returning from the dead is not so easy! He now says he [2] _____ never __________ (should /come back).

6 Canoe Death Hoax

1 Complete the article, putting the modals and verbs in brackets in the past.

2 Are the sentences true (✓) or false (✗)?

1 ☐ John said it was difficult to fake your own death.
2 ☐ The Emergency Services thought that currents had dragged John's body out to sea.
3 ☐ John's wife wasn't involved in the insurance fraud.
4 ☐ The police caught John and Anne in Panama five years later.
5 ☐ The couple's two sons had no idea that their father was alive.
6 ☐ The police never believed that the sons were involved in the insurance fraud.
7 ☐ John does not regret his actions.
8 ☐ John wishes he had stayed in Panama.

John Darwin grew a beard and travelled abroad under the name of John Jones.

Life [3] ___________ (must/be) pretty difficult for John when he decided to fake his own death. Facing imminent bankruptcy, a 'fatal accident' [4] ___________ (must/seem) a plausible way out. Indeed, everyone believed that he had accidentally fallen from his canoe into the sea near his home in County Durham. Even the Emergency Services said John [5] ___________ (can not/survive) the strong currents which [6] ______ certainly ___________ (would/drag) his body out to sea, never to be recovered.

No one [7] ___________ (could/imagine) that John was very much alive and well, and living off his £680,000 life insurance money with his wife, Anne, in Panama. However, John's conscience [8] ___________ (must/get) the better of him as five years after his disappearance, he walked into a police station in London claiming to have lost his memory.

John and Anne Darwin in their Panama flat.

At first, the police mistakenly assumed the Darwins' sons [9] ___________ (must/involve) in the scam, and they [10] ___________ (might/received) prison sentences. But John and Anne insisted that their two sons had not known their father was really alive. When they realized both their parents [11] ___________ (must/lie) to them for over four years, they were appalled.

Asked how he [12] ___________ (could/put) his own children through the trauma of thinking he had drowned, John admits that he [13] ___________ (might not/act) in their best interests, but that he had been extremely stressed.

He said, 'I [14] ___________ (should not/commit) the crime, and I [15] ___________ (should not/come back)'.

John has been accused of not showing enough remorse, but he is very philosophical. He says, 'If you don't believe it, you don't believe it!'

Vocabulary

7 Body idioms

Complete the conversations with the correct body idiom from the box.

heart-to-heart	enter your head	all fingers and thumbs
all ears	face the facts	put on a brave face
cold feet	give me a hand	hands full
out of my mind		

1

Mary Oops! Oh Clare, I'm really sorry! I've just broken your pink coffee cup. I'm [1] ____________ today.

Clare Oh, never mind. It can't be helped.

2

Jane I had a real [2] ____________ with Emily and told her exactly what we thought about her new boyfriend.

Diane Oooh! That was brave. What did you say exactly? Go on, tell me. I'm [3] ____________ .

Jane That he was a lazy waste of space, and she should stop seeing him.

3

Dad It's nearly midnight and I've been [4] ____________ with worry. Where have you been young lady?

Jo Sorry, Dad! The taxi was late bringing us back from the party.

Dad Did it never [5] ____________ to ring or at least text me?

4

Nick Hi, Jake. What's up with you? Are you all right?

Jake Well, I was supposed to be giving a talk to my English class, and at the last minute I got [6] ____________, and I just couldn't do it.

Nick Don't worry. We all get nervous about things like that.

5

Fiona Josh, can you [7] ____________ with my English assignment? I really don't understand what I'm meant to be doing?

Josh Sorry, Fiona, I've got my [8] ____________ at the moment. I've only just started writing my history essay which has to be handed in tomorrow.

6

Tina You've just got to [9] ____________ , Julie. Your marriage is over. You can't keep on finding excuses for Rob's bad behaviour.

Julie Don't you think I should just [10] ____________ for the children's sake and give him one more chance?

Tina No, I don't. Enough is enough!

Listen and check.

8 Physical appearance or personality?

1 Write these adjectives in the correct columns. Careful! One adjective can go in both columns.

~~skinny~~	moody	big-headed
brainy	graceful	wrinkled
quick-thinking	nosy	bald
cheeky	well-built	narrow-minded
affectionate	smart	curly
hard-hearted	clean-shaven	tanned

Physical appearance	Personality
skinny	

2 Complete the sentences with the parts of the body in the box, used as verbs.

arm	elbow	eye	foot	hand	head	shoulder	thumb

1 The teacher ____________ out the exam papers and told the class to begin writing.

2 I managed to ____________ my way to the front of the crowd, so I got a good view of the procession.

3 I haven't read the magazine yet, I just ____________ through it to see if there were any interesting pictures.

4 We all ____________ the new member of class with curiosity. We were eager to see what she was like.

5 They ordered the most expensive things on the menu because they knew that I'd ____________ the bill.

6 In the final seconds of the match, Benson ____________ the ball into the back of the net, making it 1–0.

7 Policemen ____________ with guns in some countries.

8 I'd hate to be Prime Minister. I don't think I could ____________ the responsibility of making so many important decisions.

Prepositions

9 Verb + preposition

Complete the sentences with a verb in its correct form and a preposition.

Verbs		Prepositions	
~~thank~~	forgive	into	of
accuse	hide	at	on
trick	hold	for	to
congratulate	inherit	from	
shout	model		
invite	remind		

1 He *thanked* the nurse *for* all her help.

2 You ________ me so much ________ your father. You look just like him.

3 Everyone ________ me ________ passing my driving test at the fourth attempt.

4 My teenage daughter ________ herself ________ her pop idol. She's had a ring put through her nose, just like him.

5 Don't ________ the truth ________ me. I want to know everything.

6 He picked up the crying baby and ________ her tightly ________ his chest.

7 We've ________ 300 guests ________ our wedding.

8 I think that TV ads ________ people ________ buying things that they don't really want.

9 I didn't ________ a penny ________ my great uncle when he died.

10 The spectators ________ abuse ________ the referee when he disallowed the goal.

11 How can I ever ________ him ________ telling me all those lies?

12 I ________ by my employers ________ stealing, which I strongly denied.

Pronunciation

10 Rhymes and limericks

1 Make rhyming pairs with the words from the box.

~~good~~	chief	court	deaf	fool	mud
height	lose	knew	knows	grieve	put
reign	nude	said	pour	weight	wool

should	/ʊd/	*good*	food	/uːd/	________
bread	/ed/	________	leaf	/iːf/	________
choose	/uːz/	________	taught	/ɔːt/	________
toes	/əʊz/	________	chef	/ef/	________
hate	/eɪt/	________	through	/uː/	________
tight	/aɪt/	________	wore	/ɔː/	________
full	/ʊl/	________	brain	/eɪn/	________
pool	/uːl/	________	leave	/iːv/	________
blood	/ʌd/	________	foot	/ʊt/	________

2 Limericks are short poems with a distinctive rhythm. The lines rhyme AABBA. Transcribe the lines written in phonetics in these two limericks.

The Pelican

A rare old bird is a pelican
His /biːk kən həʊld mɔː ðən ɪz beli kaən/

____

He /kən teɪk ɪn hɪz biːk/

____

/ɪnʌf fuːd fər ə wiːk/

____

And I'm damned if I know how the hell he can!

The Lady from Twickenham

There was a young lady from Twickenham
Whose /ʃuːz wə tuː taɪt tə wɔːk kwɪk ɪn ðəm/

____

She came back from a walk
/lʊkɪŋ waɪtə ðən tʃɔːk/

____

And she /tʊk ðəm bəʊθɒf ən wəz sɪk ɪn ðəm/

____

11

Hypothesizing • Wishes and regrets • *unless, supposing, in case*
• Similar words, different meanings • Nouns from phrasal verbs
• Ways of pronouncing *ea*

It's all hypothetical!

Real time or unreal time?

1 Real or hypothetical past?

1 These sentences all have verbs in the Past Simple. Which refer to real past time (**R**) and which are hypotheses (**H**)?

1 [R] Did you see Lorenzo when you were in Italy?
2 [H] I wish I worked in the open air.
3 [ ] If you didn't have a car, would you have to go by bus?
4 [ ] When we lived in London, we'd always travel by bus.
5 [ ] I'd rather we lived in a small country town.
6 [ ] It's time we had a new sofa.
7 [ ] If only you were always as happy as you are today.
8 [ ] Why didn't you come to the party?

2 These sentences all have verbs in the Past Perfect. Which refer to real past time (**R**) and which are hypotheses (**H**)?

1 [ ] I wish I'd said that.
2 [ ] She asked me if I had known him for a long time.
3 [ ] If I hadn't been in a meeting, I'd have taken your call.
4 [ ] If only you'd arrived five minutes earlier.
5 [ ] I woke up and realized it had all been a terrible dream.
6 [ ] What if they hadn't agreed to give you a pay rise?
7 [ ] Had the water risen a bit more, our house would have been flooded.
8 [ ] She told me she'd been given a kitten for her birthday.

3 Complete the sentences with an auxiliary verb which expresses reality.

1 I wish you didn't bite your nails, but you *do*.
2 I wish I earned more, but I __________ .
3 I should have listened to their advice, but I __________ .
4 If only I could speak Spanish, but I __________ .
5 If only he weren't so selfish, but he __________ .
6 I wish my car would start, but it __________ .
7 I wish he didn't argue all the time, but he __________ .
8 If only I hadn't been fired, but I __________ .
9 I wish I had a flat of my own, but I __________ .

Wishes and regrets

2 Present and past wishes

1 Use the words from the columns to make as many correct and logical sentences as you can.

I wish	you I	were could would had	come. rich.

____
____
____
____
____
____

2 (Circle) the correct alternative in the following sentences. Sometimes two are possible.

1 I really wish I *can / could / was able to* speak another language.
2 I wish it *wasn't / wouldn't be / isn't* so cold. I hate the winter.
3 It's time we *have / had / have had* a holiday.
4 Our holiday was a disaster. I'd rather we *didn't go / hadn't gone / weren't going*.
5 The party was brilliant after you left. You should *stay / had stayed / have stayed* longer.
6 I wish you *don't speak / didn't speak / wouldn't speak* so quickly. I can't follow you.
7 What were you doing on that wall? Supposing you*'d fallen / would fall / hadn't fallen*?
8 She'd rather her grandchildren *live / lived / had lived* nearer. Then she could see them more often.

3 Expressions of regret

1 Rewrite the sentences so they have similar meanings. Use the words in brackets.

1 I'm sorry I didn't invite him to the party. (wish)

____

2 Why weren't you watching the road? (should)

____

3 I regret saying that to her. (If only)

____

4 I shouldn't have hit him. (wish)

____

5 I don't want you to tell her. ('d rather)

____

6 I don't like it when Meg stays out so late. (wish)

____

7 I regret I didn't tell him that I loved him. (should)

____

2 Write sentences to express these people's wishes and regrets. Use the expressions from exercise 1.

1 ______________________

____

2 ______________________

____

3 ______________________

____

4 ______________________

____

5 ______________________

____

6 ______________________

____

4 What I wish I'd known ...

Read and complete the article with words from the box.

A letter to my 16-year-old self

if would hadn't should 'd

Dear Marianne,

1 _______ only I'd enjoyed my school days more and 2 _______ wished my childhood away. I 3 _______ have realized how lucky I was to be a child, a time when you have no stress, no bills, no husbands, no babies and no job! I 4 _______ have had a lot more fun if I 5 _______ just enjoyed the moment.

should only could couldn't wouldn't would

Dear George,

If 6 _______ I had known how precocious I was, I 7 _______ have been such a clever clogs! I now realize I must have really annoyed my classmates. I 8 _______ have saved up and bought some contact lenses, then I might have looked less nerdy and made more friends. I 9 _______ also have been able to see when playing rugby – a distinct advantage. I 10 _______ have done with putting on a bit of weight, too. I 11 _______ get a girlfriend because I was so skinny.

if wouldn't could imagine realized won't have unless

Dear Sue,

If I 12 _______ give you any advice, first, ignore Simon, the kid who calls you fat. 13 _______ I had 14 _______ at your age what a waste of time it is to listen to bullies, I 15 _______ have worn oversized clothes for the next four years. Just 16 _______ how he will look years from now when he's bald, then you 17 _______ feel so intimidated.
Secondly, say thank you to Mum and Dad *all* the time 18 _______ they're really nagging you about being out late.
I wouldn't 19 _______ become an actress without their support.
So, 16-year-old me, give them the biggest hug – they deserve it!
Looking back, I wish I could!

Third conditional

5 Regrets

1 Below are the top five regrets in life. Read the article quickly. Which regret goes with which paragraph? Write them in.

'I wish I had said what I was really thinking.' 'I wish I hadn't worked so hard!' 'I wish I had been true to myself.' 'I wish I had done more!' 'I wish we had stayed in touch.'

Top five regrets in life

As we progress through our lives, we sometimes pause and ponder on what might have been and how the choices, decisions, and behaviour from our past have affected who we are today. Hindsight gives us a clearer vision of what we should have done, and we can't help but wonder what we would change about our past actions if we could do it all again! Here are our top five regrets.

1 ____________________

Too often we live our lives trying to please other people rather than fulfilling our own dreams. Many of us wish we had made braver choices, ones that would have allowed us to follow our real passion in life. Many of us believe that if we hadn't always chosen to please other people, we would have very different lives, jobs, or partners today.

2 ____________________

Many of us who are parents realize as we get older that the treadmill of work has been a barrier to spending enough quality time with our children. We wonder whether it was really necessary to stay so late at work, and we feel sad that we can never claim back their childhood. If we hadn't spent so much time at the office, we might have more happy memories of playing with our kids and reading bedtime stories. Children grow up quickly!

3 ____________________

Too often we suppress our feelings to keep the peace and are too scared to say what we really feel. As a result, we end up feeling resentful, which drains our energy. In the past, if we had said what we truly believed, we wouldn't now feel bitter and full of regret. It's never too late, though. Be strong and say what you feel (within reason) and you will find you have more positive energy in your life.

4 ____________________

Established friendships are crucial for our mental well-being. Unfortunately, too many of us lose contact with old friends. One of our top five regrets is the loss of golden friendships that have slipped away over the years because we were too busy. So, although social networking sites like Facebook and Twitter make it easier to stay in touch these days, it takes more than a status update, a quick text, or a tweet to keep a good friendship on track.

5 ____________________

Many of us do not realize that we could have been happier if we'd moved outside of our comfort zone. Instead, we got stuck in familiar routines and forgot to look around for new opportunities. When we look back at our actions, we often wish we had taken risks and been more fulfilled. Just think, if we hadn't compromised with the safe option, you might have experienced more in your life and had a lot more fun!

2 Complete these third conditional regrets with information from the text. Which regret do they go with?

1 If I hadn't always put my work first, I could have __________ with my children. ☐

2 I would have had more fun in my life if I __________ more risks. ☐

3 I wouldn't feel bitter now if I hadn't __________ to say what I really feel. ☐

4 I'd have many more friends now if I'd __________ with them over the years. ☐

5 If only I hadn't tried to please other people all the time, I would have __________ my own dreams. ☐

3 Rearrange the words to make excuses in the third conditional.

1. wouldn't / been / if / ill / hadn't / shellfish / had / I / I / have / the
2. phoned / had / had / if / you / have / time / would / I / the / I
3. if / known / had / I / the jumper / machine-washable / wasn't / wouldn't / I / bought / have / it
4. if / it / own / my / eyes / seen / with / hadn't / I / wouldn't / believed / I / have / it

4 Complete the second sentence to express the excuse in a different way.

1. I didn't know you had a mobile. I didn't contact you.

   If I'd known you had a mobile, I could/would have contacted you.
2. I didn't send you a postcard because I didn't know your address.

   If I ______________________________ a postcard.
3. I didn't remember when your birthday was. That's why I didn't buy you a present.

   If ______________________________.
4. I broke the speed limit because I was rushing my wife to the hospital.

   If ______________________________.
5. I'm sorry I'm late. I forgot to set my alarm clock.

   If ______________________________.

All conditionals

6 Revision of all conditionals

Put the verb in brackets in the correct tense to form either the first, second, third, or zero conditional. There are also some examples of mixed conditionals.

1. If I still __________ (feel) sick, I __________ (not go) on holiday next weekend.
2. You make such delicious chocolate cakes! If you __________ (sell) them, you __________ (make) a fortune.
3. Hello, Liz. Are you still looking for Pat? If I __________ (see) her, I __________ (tell) her you want to speak to her.
4. If Alice __________ (go) to Exeter University, she __________ (not met) her husband, Andrew.
5. **A** Does she love him?

   B Of course she does. If she __________ (not love) him, she __________ (not marry) him.
6. If you __________ (buy) two bottles of shampoo, you __________ (get) one free.
7. **A** What __________ you __________ (do) if you __________ (see) a ghost?

   B I __________ (run) away!
8. If we __________ (bring) the map with us, we __________ (not be) lost.
9. You are lucky to be alive. If you __________ (not have) a smoke alarm, the house __________ (burn down) with you in it.
10. You were very rude to Max. If I __________ (be) you, I __________ (apologize).
11. Ashley is allergic to cheese. If he __________ (eat) it, he __________ (get) a rash.
12. We've run out of petrol. If you __________ (listen) to me, you __________ (hear) me saying that we were running low. Then we __________ (not be) stuck here now.

Ways of introducing conditionals

1 Conditionals can be introduced in a variety of ways other than with *if*.

unless

Unless means *except if*.

> *We'll go swimming* ***unless*** *it rains.*
>
> ***Unless*** *there's a strike, I'll be at work tomorrow.*

in case

In case means the first action is a precaution: it happens because the second action *might* happen.

> *I'll take my umbrella* ***in case*** *it rains.*
>
> *Take your boots* ***in case*** *it's muddy.*

Supposing ... / Suppose ... / Imagine ...

These mean the same as *Imagine if ... ?* or *What if ... ?*

They are questions, and they come at the beginning of a sentence.

> ***Supposing*** *you could go on holiday tomorrow, where would you go?*
>
> ***Imagine*** *you were rich, what would you buy?*

2 In more formal styles, *if* can be dropped and the auxiliary verb inverted. This is common with *had*, *were*, and *should*.

> ***Were*** *they my children, I wouldn't let them watch so much TV.* (If they were my children ...)
>
> ***Had I known*** *that he was a journalist, I would have said nothing.* (If I had known ...)
>
> ***Should*** *the meeting* ***overrun****, I'll have to cancel my dinner engagement.* (If the meeting should overrun ...)

7 Words other than *if*

1 (Circle) the correct word to complete the sentence.

1 *In case / Imagine* there were no more wars – wouldn't that be wonderful?
2 I'm going to take a cushion to the concert, *in case / unless* the seats are hard.
3 We'll miss the beginning of the film *if / unless* you hurry.
4 *Unless / In case* you behave yourself, you can't come to the party with us.
5 *Suppose / Should* you got lost, what would you do?
6 I'll take a book *in case / unless* I'm bored on the journey.
7 *Had / Supposing* I understood the problem, I'd have done something about it.
8 *Should / In case* you fail to pay this bill, court action will be taken.

2 Rewrite these sentences using the words in brackets.

1 I won't come if they don't invite me. (unless)

2 What would you do if he left you? (supposing)

3 If you had learned to play tennis, would you have been a champion by now? (suppose)

4 We're going to install a smoke alarm. There may be a fire. (in case)

5 She won't get that job if she doesn't learn to speak French. (unless)

6 If the lifeguard hadn't been there, what would have happened? (imagine)

7 I won't go out this evening. Justin might ring. (in case)

8 I'll be at my desk until 6.00 if you need to speak to me about the matter. (should)

Vocabulary

8 Similar words, different meaning

These adjective pairs are easy to confuse. Complete the sentences with the correct adjectives.

unreadable illegible

1 I couldn't work out who the letter was from. The signature was completely ___________ .

2 I know Shakespeare is very popular, but I find him totally ___________ .

childish childlike

3 Manisha is so ___________ . She's always having temper tantrums.

4 It was wonderful to watch the lambs playing. I got such ___________ pleasure from it.

sensible sensitive

5 Sophie is extremely ___________ at the moment. Anything you say upsets her.

6 Fabienne is not a very ___________ person. She wore high-heeled shoes for our four-mile walk.

true truthful

7 I've never known her to tell a lie. She's a very ___________ person.

8 I can never watch sad films that are based on a ___________ story. They always make me cry.

intolerable intolerant

9 Susan is so ___________ of other people. She never accepts anyone else's opinion, and she always thinks she knows best.

10 I find Marek's behaviour ___________ . It's unfair to be so selfish.

economic economical

11 We're in ___________ crisis at the moment. James has lost his job and I don't know how we are going to pay the mortgage.

12 It's much more ___________ to drive slowly. You get more kilometres for your money.

Phrasal verbs

9 Nouns from phrasal verbs

1 There are many nouns formed from phrasal verbs. Sometimes the verb comes first, sometimes second.

__make__-up *down__fall__* *up__bringing__*
__draw__back *out__break__* *__take__away*

2 Sometimes the noun is related to the phrasal verb.

I don't use much __make-up__.
She __made up__ her face very carefully. = related

Sometimes they are not related.

The main __drawback__ is the cost. (drawback = disadvantage)
__Draw back__ the curtains and let the sunshine in. (draw back = open)

Complete these sentences with the nouns in the box.

outcome	breakthrough	outbreak	takeaway
check-up	breakdown	comeback	feedback
outlook	downfall		

1 The ___________ of communication between management and workers means the strike will continue.

2 His career has suffered recently, but with a new album and a world tour, he's determined to make a ___________ .

3 I go to the dentist twice a year for a ___________ .

4 The ___________ of the local elections is that the Green party has won 12 new seats.

5 The weather should be fine over the next few days, and the ___________ for the weekend is warm and sunny.

6 There has been an ___________ of salmonella, infecting 83 people in just over two weeks.

7 There has been a significant ___________ in the search to find a cure for breast cancer.

8 Online companies often ask customers for ___________ because it is a quick, cheap way of doing market research.

9 We're having an Indian ___________ for supper.

10 He used to be a highly successful athlete, but taking too many drugs was his ___________ .

Listening

10 Homeless to Harvard

1 Listen to Clare trying to inspire her son, Harry, to study harder. Match a question in **A** with an answer in **B**.

A	B
1 ☐ When does Harry have his exams?	a Because she had two young children.
2 ☐ Why was it difficult for Clare to study for her degree?	b Because she nags him.
3 ☐ Why does Harry get irritated with his mother?	c On the Internet.
4 ☐ Where did Clare find out about Liz Murray?	d Next month.
5 ☐ What did Liz and her sister sometimes eat for their dinner?	e Toothpaste.
6 ☐ Who does Liz now give speeches with?	f She's an author and speaker.
7 ☐ How old was Liz when her mother died?	g 15.
8 ☐ What did Liz's mother always believe?	h Bill Clinton.
9 ☐ How did Liz afford to go to Harvard?	i One day life is going to get better.
10 ☐ What does Liz do now?	j She got a scholarship from *The New York Times*.

2 Listen again. Match the lines to make sentences.

1 If Harry does more revision,	a she would have got her degree sooner.
2 If Clare had worked harder at school,	b she wouldn't have died so young.
3 If Liz's mother hadn't been a drug addict,	c he might do better in his exams.
4 If Liz hadn't gone to night classes,	d she wouldn't have completed her high school education.
5 If Liz's teacher hadn't taken her to Harvard,	e he might regret it one day.
6 If Harry spends all his time on the PlayStation,	f she may never have considered studying there.

3 Listen again. Who says these things, Clare (**C**) or Harry (**H**)?

1 I wasted so many years just watching TV. ☐
2 Give me a break. ☐
3 You just don't realize how lucky you are. ☐
4 ... and you think I'm bad. ☐
5 That is desperate. ☐
6 ... she never forgot her mother's mantra ☐
7 You've made your point. ☐

4 Look at the tapescript on p86 and check your answers.

Pronunciation

11 Ways of pronouncing *ea*

1 There are several different ways of pronouncing the letters *ea*. Look at the examples in the columns below.

/e/	/iː/	/ɪə/
bread	meat	fear

/eə/	/eɪ/	/ɜː/
wear	break	learn

2 Put these words into the correct column according to the pronunciation of *ea*.

dear	thread	pearl	leap
tear (n)	bear	pear	leapt
tear (v)	cheat	heal	meant
scream	clear	health	reason
steak	deaf	great	search
breath	death	gear	swear
breathe	earth	jealous	theatre
breadth	beast	lead (v)	weary
hear	beard	lead (n)	weapon

12

Articles • Determiners • Demonstratives • Nouns in groups • *be* and *have* • Emphasis in speaking

Time flies

Articles

1 *a, the,* or zero article?

1 Complete the sentences with *a*, *the*, or nothing (zero article).

1 Excuse me! Is there ______ bank near here?

2 **A** I haven't got any money.
B I'm going to ______ bank. I'll get you some.

3 Has ______ postman been this morning?

4 My brother works as ______ postman.

5 We've seen a house we want to move to. It's got ______ views over fields, and there's ______ lovely garden at ______ back.

6 **A** Where's Nick?
B In ______ garden.

7 I bought ______ dog to protect myself against ______ burglars.

8 Tony joined ______ Police Dog Unit because he likes working with ______ dogs.

9 We went out for ______ meal last night. ______ food was excellent. I don't usually like ______ Chinese food, but ______ duck was superb.

2 Complete the newspaper article with *a*, *an*, *the*, or nothing.

It's never too early

Abha, 7, gains her GCSE in computing

[1] ______ girl aged seven went into *The Guinness Book of Records* yesterday when she became [2] ______ youngest pupil ever to pass [3] ______ national exam.

Abha Subramanian, from Manchester, studied at [4] ______ Ellesmere College near her home several evenings [5] ______ week, finally gaining [6] ______ grade C in [7] ______ computer studies and earning a place in [8] ______ record books.

She says: 'I think [9] ______ computers are easy but [10] ______ exam was quite hard.' She praised her teacher, James Nolan, [11] ______ founder and principal of [12] ______ college. 'He's [13] ______ nice teacher – he tells us [14] ______ jokes!'

Dr Nolan commented: 'You must have [15] ______ faith in children. They can make [16] ______ paper planes one minute and write [17] ______ computer program [18] ______ next. [19] ______ pupils at my school aren't prodigies – they are just interested and motivated. They are [20] ______ example of what [21] ______ rest of [22] ______ country could be doing.

It is Dr Nolan's firm belief that age 18 is already too old for [23] ______ university and [24] ______ academic world. He maintains that students of this age have passed their mental peak.

Determiners

2 *all* and *every*

1 Circle the correct answer.

1. Anna is such a show-off, she thinks she knows *all* / *everything*.
2. My driving test was a complete disaster. *All* / *Everything* went wrong.
3. Kate didn't say where she was going. *All* / *Everything* she said was that she was going out.
4. *All* / *Every* child in the class failed the exam.
5. *All* / *Everything* I want for my birthday is to lie in bed until midday.
6. I'm starving. *All* / *Everything* I've eaten today is a packet of crisps.
7. I really don't get on with my new boss. I disagree with *all* / *everything* she says.
8. I can't go higher than £500 for the car. That's *everything* / *all* I can afford.
9. Megan couldn't believe her luck. *All* / *Every* topic she had revised the night before came up in the exam.
10. The film was so boring that *all* / *everybody* fell asleep.

2 Circle the correct answer.

1. I have three dogs. *All* / *Every* of them love going for a walk, but *neither* / *none* of them likes being brushed.
2. You can borrow *either* / *each* the Renault or the Volvo. They're *all* / *both* in the garage.
3. My two daughters are *each* / *both* good at languages, but *none* / *neither* of them can do maths at all.
4. I have a shower *every* / *each* day.
5. I have *any* / *no* idea how I spend all my money. At the end of *every* / *either* month, it's all gone.
6. I know *every* / *each* word of his songs by heart.
7. There are 15 rooms in this hotel. *Each* / *Every* room is a little different.
8. You can have *either* / *each* an orange or an apple, but you can't have *either* / *both*.
9. **A** Tea or coffee?
   B *Either* / *Neither*, thanks. I've got to rush.
10. **A** Red wine or white?
    B *Either* / *Neither*, whichever is open.
11. I know *either* / *both* Robert and his brother, but I don't like *both* / *either* of them.
12. I have four brothers. *Every* / *Each* of us is different.

Demonstratives

3 *this, that, these, those*

Put *this*, *that*, *these*, or *those* into each gap.

1. ___________ shoes are killing me. I can't wait to take them off.
2. (On the phone) Hello. ___________ is Beth. Can I speak to Kate?
3. ___________ was a wonderful film, wasn't it?
4. I knew Jenny at university. In ___________ days, she had long blonde hair.
5. **A** Anything else?
   B No, ___________'s all for today, thanks.
6. Well, ___________'ll be £5.50, please.
7. I can't get ___________ ring off my finger. It's stuck.
8. You just can't get proper sausages ___________ days.
9. Come here and tidy up ___________ mess right now!
10. Listen to ___________. It says in the paper that life's been found on Mars.
11. Did you ever hear from ___________ girl you met on holiday last year?
12. I was in the pub last night when ___________ bloke came up to me and hit me.
13. **A** I got a parking fine today.
    B ___________'ll teach you a lesson.
14. Who were ___________ people you were talking to last night?
15. What was ___________ noise? Didn't you hear it?

Revision of articles, determiners, and demonstratives

4 Searching for Sugar Man

Complete the article about the documentary *Searching for Sugar Man* with the words in the boxes. Each word can be used once only.

Searching for Sugar Man

RODRIGUEZ – one of the greatest 70s rock icons – but it took the world over 40 years to discover him!

a couple of	the (x 2)	his	little
a great deal of	this	several	enough

Rodriguez was first discovered in Detroit, Michigan, in [1] __________ late 60s by [2] __________ well-known music producers who were struck by [3] __________ touching music and expressive lyrics. There was [4] __________ anticipation when he recorded his first album, *Cold Fact*, in 1970. It included his best-known song, 'Sugar Man'. [5] __________ song earned [6] __________ good reviews and Rodriguez was compared to Bob Dylan. Unfortunately, this wasn't [7] __________ of a recommendation to ensure its success, and [8] __________ album bombed in the US. A second album, *Coming from Reality*, also had [9] __________ success in the US, and Rodriguez disappeared into obscurity.

every	no	the	a	many of	both	this

However, unbeknown to him, Rodriguez' two albums had arrived in South Africa where [10] __________ of them had become hugely popular in the 1970s. [11] __________ success was mainly because the powerful music and lyrics reflected so well the message of the anti-apartheid movement of the time. Despite there being [12] __________ promotion at all on [13] __________ radio, word of the albums spread, and over half a million records were sold. Nearly [14] __________ student in South Africa owned [15] __________ copy of *Cold Fact*. Rodriguez' music influenced a generation of fans, just as Jimi Hendrix's songs had become important to [16] __________ the US troops in Vietnam.

the	some	more	anything
nobody	a wealth of	his	

Over the next two decades, his popularity grew. Rodriguez had [17] __________ fans than Elvis Presley and the Beatles, but [18] __________ knew who he was or [19] __________ else about him. There were even [20] __________ rumours that he had taken [21] __________ own life whilst on stage! This was, of course, before the advent of [22] __________ Internet. Today, a search on Google would have quickly uncovered [23] __________ information.

the	a	an	one	most	these	all

The riddle of Rodriguez is what the documentary film *Searching for Sugar Man* sets out to solve. After years of searching, Swedish director Malek Bendjelloul finally discovered the singer-songwriter alive and well, and still living in Detroit, where he worked as [24] __________ builder and had brought up three daughters. It was [25] __________ of [26] __________ daughters who filled in [27] __________ of the blanks about his life.

There is now [28] __________ official Sugar Man website. His albums have been re-released and are available to his fans [29] __________ over the world, and *Searching for Sugar Man* won Best Documentary in [30] __________ 2013 Oscars.

Nouns in groups

1 There are three main ways that we can put nouns together.

noun + noun	noun + 's + noun
post office	*my wife's sister*
headache	*the doctor's surgery*
face-lift	*the dog's bowl*

noun + preposition + noun
the end of the garden
a story about compassion
the arrival of the police

2 Sometimes more than one structure can be used.

the Prime Minister's arrival
the arrival of the Prime Minister
the floor of the living room
the living room floor
the car door handle
the handle on the car door

But usually only one pattern is possible.

the back of the car

NOT ~~the car back~~ ~~the car's back~~

3 Sometimes there is a change in meaning.

the cat's food = the food that belongs to one particular cat
The dog has eaten the ***cat's food****.*
cat food = food for cats in general
Can you buy some more ***cat food*** *when you go out?*

IT'S A NEW FLAVOR, HENRY. HE WANTS YOU TO TRY IT FIRST.
CAT FOOD

4 We use the noun + noun pattern (compound nouns) for everyday established combinations.

a love film, a horror film

For less established combinations, we prefer noun + preposition + noun.

a film about horses

NOT ~~*a horse film*~~

5 Combining nouns

Combine the words in brackets using one of the three patterns. Sometimes there is more than one answer.

1 Your coat's on the ____________ (back, chair).
2 You've just spilt the ____________ (milk, cat).
3 Can you buy some ____________ (paper, toilet)? We've run out.
4 I never listened to my ____________ (advice, parents).
5 Can you buy a ____________ (wine, bottle) to have with dinner?
6 What did that ____________ (road, sign) say? Did you see it?
7 It's such a mess in here. There are empty ____________ (wine, bottles) everywhere.
8 The ____________ (Prime Minister, duties) include entertaining heads of state.
9 The ____________ (my shoe, heel) has come off.
10 Can I borrow your ____________ (brush, hair)?
11 What happened at the ____________ (film, end)?
12 Here is ____________ (today, news).
13 Where is the nearest ____________ (Underground, station)?
14 It's my ____________ (anniversary, parents, wedding) next week.
15 The ____________ (company, success) is due to its efficiency.
16 I've got a ____________ (fortnight, holiday) next month.
17 The ____________ (government, economic policy) is confusing.
18 The annual ____________ (rate, inflation) is about 4%.
19 Are there any ____________ (coffee, cups) in your bedroom? There are none in the kitchen.
20 Do you want a ____________ (coffee, cup)?

Vocabulary

6 Hot verbs – *be*, *have*

1 Match the words and expressions with *be* or *have*. Tick (✔) the correct column.

be	have	
✔		fed up with sb/sth
	✔	the right to do sth
		the nerve to do sth
		on the safe side
		in touch with sb
		a word with sb
		no point in doing sth
		on one's mind
		up to date
		no chance of doing sth

2 Complete the sentences with one of the expressions from exercise 1 in the correct form.

1 My job is so boring. I'm really fed up with it.

2 If you don't like your meal, you ___________ complain to the manager.

3 Thank you for your interview, Miss Clarke. We ___________ you as soon as we've made a decision about the job.

4 I can't stop thinking about my ex-girlfriend. She ___________ always ___________ .

5 Mrs Bennett! Can I ___________ you for a minute? It's about your son Ben.

6 Jack was so cheeky! He ___________ tell me that this dress didn't suit me!

7 I've got extra holiday insurance just in case. I always like ___________ .

8 Well, I'll apply for the manager's job, but I know I ___________ getting it.

9 Wait here. If you don't like heights, there ___________ climbing up the tower with us.

10 In my job, it is important to ___________ with what's going on in the financial market.

Prepositions revision

7 Noun + preposition

Complete the sentences with a preposition or a combination of prepositions.

1 After running up the stairs, I was ___________ breath.

2 You make some silly mistakes, but ___________ general, your work has been good.

3 I went on holiday ___________ my own, because sometimes I like to be ___________ myself.

4 I got a cheque ___________ £500 in the post.

5 There has been a rise ___________ the number of violent crimes.

6 The difference ___________ you and me is that I don't mind hard work.

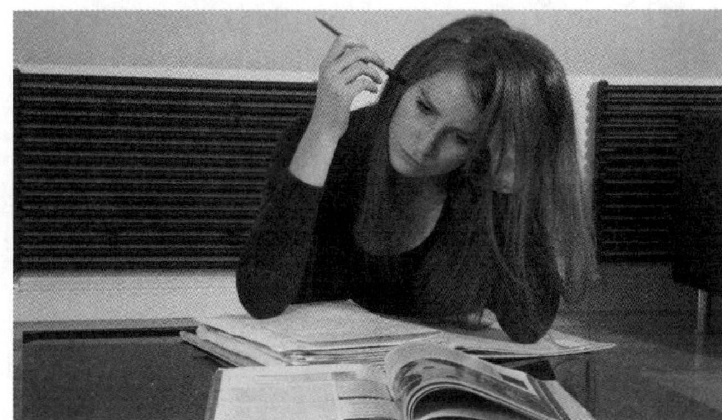

7 I can think of no reason ___________ her strange behaviour.

8 It took a long time to find a solution ___________ the problem.

9 I need some information ___________ global warming.

10 I'm having trouble ___________ my car. It won't start in the mornings.

11 In the accident, there was quite a bit of damage ___________ my car.

12 Investigators are trying to find the cause ___________ the accident.

13 I've got to do my homework ___________ tomorrow.

14 I don't see James any more. I haven't been ___________ touch with him for years.

15 Did you get an invitation ___________ David's wedding?

Listening

8 You're never too old

1 Listen to Mary Hobson talking about her life. Mark the statements true (✓) or false (✗).

1 ☐ She wrote a book before she was 40.
2 ☐ She took care of her sick husband.
3 ☐ She didn't read all of *War and Peace*.
4 ☐ She learnt Russian from an old lady.
5 ☐ The happiest time of her life was in the 1960s.
6 ☐ Recently, she's started to lose her memory.
7 ☐ She loves Moscow but isn't crazy about the cold weather.
8 ☐ She plans to continue learning Greek.

2 Listen again and complete these lines with the exact words from the text.

1 I am what __________________ a late developer.
2 We were ______________________________, we lived on national assistance.
3 _______________________ was his fault, of course.
4 Then it ________________________________: I hadn't read it at all, I'd only read a translation,
5 _________ the town _________ the country any day.
6 I won't be able to _________________________ forever.
7 When I can't ____________________________ my front steps, I'll perfect my Greek.
8 ___________________ I have my books, I'll be happy.

3 There is one mistake in each of these sentences. Find it and correct it.

1 Mary was 62 when she went to ~~a~~ university.
2 Her husband was talented jazz musician.
3 She believes that you've only got a life so you mustn't waste it.
4 Mary decided to learn the Russian and Greek.
5 She read the all of *War and Peace* in Russian.
6 She prefers the town over a countryside.
7 She loves lying in the bed listening to the snow.
8 He lost the speech and the use of the right side of his body.

Pronunciation

9 Nouns and verbs

In the chart the nouns end in an unvoiced sound (/s/, /f/, /θ/), and the verbs end in a voiced sound (/z/, /v/, /ð/).

Complete the chart with the words and the phonetics. The vowel sound or the spelling changes.

Noun		Verb	
advice			/əd'vaɪz/
		to use	
abuse			
	/bɪ'liːf/		
			/rɪ'liːv/
grief			
	/ɪk'skjuːs/		
breath			
		to halve	
	/haʊs/		
safe			
			/beɪð/

10 Emphasis in speaking

Mark where the main stress is in **B**'s replies. Listen, check, and repeat.

1 **A** Why didn't you do your homework last night?
B I <u>did</u> do it.

2 **A** Who made this mark on the carpet?
B I did it. Sorry.

3 **A** Did you know that Johann and Maria are coming tonight?
B I knew Johann was coming.

4 **A** Did you know that Johann and Maria are coming tonight?
B I knew that ages ago.

5 **A** Who told Gran that I crashed her car?
B I didn't tell her.

6 **A** I wish you hadn't told Gran I crashed her car.
B I didn't tell her.

7 **A** I lost all my money playing cards.
B I told you.

8 **A** You don't like Mike and Annie, do you?
B I like Annie.

9 **A** Why don't you like Annie?
B I do like Annie. I think she's great.

10 **A** I feel so sorry for Annie. Nobody likes her.
B I like her.

Tapescripts

UNIT 1

Exercise 11, parts 1 and 2

Missing home

N = Nancy A = Amy

N Hi, Amy! Phew … Just finished my first assignment – I hope it's okay. Fancy tea and cake in my room to celebrate? It's one of my mum's homemade chocolate cakes. She brought it with her when she came to visit last weekend.

A Sure! Always got time for cake. I haven't had any home-cooked food for ages. I've been living off chips from the college canteen!

N Eugh! Those chips are so greasy! I really miss home-cooked food – my dad's chicken curry, and my mum's apple pie. I can't be bothered to cook for myself.

A Know what you mean. It's too much effort to cook for one. Mmm! This cake is great! Tastes yummy. I was so looking forward to university, but now I'm here I feel homesick.

N You, too? Thought it was just me. Everyone else seems to be having such a good time, but I feel quite lonely.

A I know how you feel. I'm missing all my friends from home. It takes time to get to know people.

N My flatmates are out partying most nights. I've always been quite happy staying in, having friends round, and watching TV.

A Me, too! Can't really do that here as our rooms are so small. I miss having a whole house to walk around in. And have you seen the state of the communal kitchen? It's gross!

N Yes. Students aren't the tidiest. I suppose we're not used to looking after ourselves.

A I must admit, I do like the independence – no one asking what time you'll be home.

N And we also get to eat as much chocolate cake as we want! Want some more?

UNIT 2

Exercise 7, parts 1, 2 and 3

Off the beaten track

P = Presenter KM = Kay Morris VS = Vicky Smith GB = Gary

P Welcome to *Off the Beaten Track*. Today I am joined by Kay Morris, a tour operator, Vicky Smith, a travel writer, and Gary Braithwaite, a film director who has filmed in some breathtaking locations. Good morning, everyone!

KM, VS, GB Good morning!

P Now, Kay, you're here to tell us about your most recent excursion.

KM Yes, I'm always looking for adventurous holiday experiences for my clients, so I was thrilled when I was invited to stay in an eco-lodge in the Ecuadorian Amazon, owned and run by the legendary Huaorani Tribe. I've been travelling for over 30 years, but meeting the Huaorani people was a totally new experience. Nothing could have prepared me for the enthusiastic welcome we received – truly amazing. We spent our days on silent rivers in dugout canoes fishing, and learning tricks of survival in the rainforest. In the evenings, we sat with the villagers around a crackling fire eating the food we'd caught and exchanging stories about our different lives. This is the perfect destination for people who are looking for a completely different holiday.

P Thank you, Kay! Now my next guest is Vicky Smith, a travel writer who has written a series of books for the more adventurous tourist. Her latest book focuses on places to stay, and as she discovered, there are interesting alternatives to five-star hotels! Could you tell us, Vicky, about one place that stands out for you?

VS There are so many enchanting places to stay in around the world. However, the most memorable for me was a bed and breakfast in Vienna. At first, I was staying in a five-star hotel – it was supposedly a romantic haunt for spies and celebrities – but for £250 a night, it had the atmosphere of an airport lounge and not a James Bond lookalike to be seen! So, I gathered my luggage and went to 'The Rooms', a family run B and B in the centre of Vienna. I was shown into a comfortable room with a sunlit terrace and stunning views of the city, its cathedrals, and church towers. For only £60 a night, I had a great breakfast, the cleanest facilities, and the friendliest atmosphere I've ever experienced in all my travels. It really does pay to look around for alternative accommodation.

P Well, thank you, Vicky! And our final guest today is Gary Braithwaite, a film director from New Zealand. You spend a lot of time, Gary, searching for the right locations to add authenticity to your films. Why is this?

GB The location is just so crucial to the atmosphere of the movie. And having grown up in the middle of nowhere in a small town in New Zealand, I've always craved adventure. I needed a real American experience to inspire me for my latest film, so I decided to visit the largest Native American reservation in the US, the Navajo Nation, which extends across the boundaries of Arizona, Utah, and New Mexico. It's like a separate country; it has its own flag, time zone, and language. It was here that I found the America I had imagined from thousands of miles away in New Zealand. I powwowed with the other men, rode horses bareback, and rounded up cattle. This experience really influenced my movie. Forget Disneyland! If you want a true American adventure, visit the Navajo Nation.

P How interesting! Thank you, and thank you to all my guests! I hope you'll tune in again next week.

UNIT 3

Exercise 9, parts 1 and 2

It's complicated!

J = **Julie** **A** = **Amy**

J Hi, Amy! Did you have a good weekend?

A Yes, thanks, Julie! Taylor and I just lazed about all Sunday afternoon reading the papers. Actually, I read a really interesting article in *The Sunday Times* – it reminded me of Linda and Graham.

J Did it? Why was that?

A Well, it was all about how the hatred between divorced couples can sometimes, over time, develop into love again.

J Really?

A Yeah! You know, like in that film a few years back. What was it called? It had Meryl Streep and Alec Baldwin in it. It was about a divorced couple who got back together.

J Oh, yes, I think it was called 'It's complicated'. Steve Martin was in it, too. It was really funny.

A Yes, that was it – 'It's Complicated'. Well, you know how in the film Alec Baldwin starts yearning for his old life with his ex-wife, Meryl Streep. You know, because she shares his memories and she's the mother of his children, and she knows how to cook his favourite food and ...

J Yeah, and the novelty of his new, young wife has worn off and ...

A Yes! And he's exhausted trying to keep up with her!

J Anyway, this article was saying how many divorced couples can become best friends again because they have their memories and so many things in common.

J Actually, I can believe that. So, what about Linda and Graham? They've been divorced for ages.

A Exactly!

J Surely they're not back together? They couldn't stand each other!

A Well, you really won't believe this! They met again at Linda's grandma's funeral last week. Graham and the grandma had always got along really well. Anyhow, they started reminiscing, and all the animosity just slipped away.

J Ah! That's lovely.

A I think they realized how much they had in common, and that perhaps they'd not worked hard enough at their marriage, and they've started dating again.

J They haven't! That's amazing! I hope it works out for them.

A Yes, me too! I really like them both.

J You know, I think we sometimes give up on things too easily. You have to work hard at relationships.

A That's very true! Fingers crossed about Linda and Graham. It would be such a happy ending.

UNIT 4

Exercise 8, part 1

Not the whole truth!

1

Lauren Hi, Susie! Do you like my dress? I bought it especially for the party. It cost an absolute fortune.

Susie It really suits you, and it's a lovely colour. It really hugs your figure.

2

David Happy Birthday, Alan! How old are you now?

Alan Forty-two! Can you believe it?

David No way! You don't look a day over 25!

3

Officer Do you know you were driving at 100 mph?

Charlie Sorry, officer! I had no idea how fast I was going.

4

Wife How come you're home so late? Where have you been? I told you I would have dinner ready for seven o'clock!

Husband Honey, I'm so sorry! I had a meeting with my boss and it finished late.

5

Tom Wow ... saucepans … thanks, Mum. What a useful birthday present!

Mum Well, I thought that now you've moved in to your own flat, you can start cooking for your friends and for me when I visit!

Tom A brilliant present, Mum! Just what I've always wanted!

6

Fiona Isn't he the cutest? They say you always think your own baby is beautiful, but in this case he really is.

Beth You must be so proud. He's adorable … looks just like his dad.

7

Pat Could we have the bill, please?

Waiter Of course, Madam! I'll just get it for you.

Peter Oh no! I don't believe it! I'll have to pay next time. I seem to have come out without my wallet.

8

Alistair I hope you like the chicken vindaloo. I've never cooked it before, and thought it might be too hot.

Colin It's delicious. Nice and spicy. I won't have any more, thank you. I'm rather full.

UNIT 5

Exercise 4, parts 1 and 2

Future Continuous or Future Perfect?

J = **Jack** **T** = **Tommy** **M** = **Millie**

J Do you ever wonder what you'll be doing in ten years' time?

T Yeah! I think about it all the time. I'll be 25, and I'll be Captain Tommy Devoy, and I'll be flying A380s for British Airways.

J Says you! How can you be so sure?

T Oh, I can see it now – I'll be based at Heathrow, and I'll be living in London, flying to far-off countries like Singapore, Hong Kong, Brazil and ...

J Huh! You'd better fly to New York, too, Tommy, because that's where I'll be living. I'll be in a deluxe apartment on Fifth Avenue, in the heart of Manhattan.

T So, what will you be doing in New York?

J I'm going to be a lawyer for one of the best law firms in New York City.

T Ugh! Law's boring.

M Well, I don't understand you two at all. What's so great about living in a big city? It's just millions of people rushing around. By the time I'm 30, I'll be living somewhere really beautiful and peaceful in the north of England, like the Lake District, and by then, I'll have saved enough money to buy a lovely, big, old farmhouse, and I'll have lots of animals.

J It sounds grim to me. I'd go mad living in the country. Give me the city life any time. While you're chatting to sheep and pigs, I'll be partying with celebrities.

T Yeah, I'm with Jack on this. And, anyway, Millie, how come you'll have enough money to buy a farmhouse?

M From my swimming, of course! I'm aiming to swim for Great Britain at the next Olympics, and I'll be an Olympic medallist. And, after I've become famous, I'll design my own brand of swimwear and make enough money to buy my farmhouse.

T To be an Olympic medallist, you'll have to give up on the rest of life and train from morning 'til night.

M Yeah, I know. That's OK by me.

J But I'll be going to the coolest clubs in New York. And by the time I'm 30, I'll have married a rich film star who will love city life as much as me, and we'll be living in a huge, swanky apartment overlooking Central Park.

M Well, that's not my kind of life.

T And by the time I'm 30, I'll be living in a penthouse flat in London overlooking the River Thames with a gorgeous girlfriend who earns a fortune in the city.

M Huh! In your dreams, Tommy! You'll be lucky to get a girlfriend at all by the time you're 30, let alone a rich, pretty one.

T Hey, watch it, Millie! The girls will be queuing up for me. You'll see!

UNIT 6

Exercise 11, parts 1 and 2

A job interview

I = interviewer J = Jane

I Good morning, Jane! Please take a seat.
J Thank you!
I Did it take you long to get here today?
J No, I live near Bristol so it was less than thirty minutes, and there was very little traffic.
I Good! So, tell me a bit about yourself, and what you can offer Perfect Petfood Ltd.
J Well, I've always loved animals. I had a horse when I was a girl, and we always had lots of dogs and cats at home. I knew from a young age I wanted to work with animals. I also have excellent people skills and a confident personality, which makes me an ideal candidate to promote your high quality pet food products. I am passionate about providing the best for animals.
I Do you know much about our company?
J Well, I have looked on your website and see that you believe in providing only the best quality products for animals, and you are one of the few pet food companies that have organic food for dogs and cats. The organic range is a market bestseller endorsed by several high-profile celebrity pet owners.
I You seem to know a great deal about our company. Could you give me some more information on your key skills and strengths? How is your previous experience relevant to this position?
J Well, I know it's a different field, but I was top sales person for the beauty department at Selfridges, London. In your job description, you ask for someone who shows initiative, is resourceful, and self-confident. In my previous role, I was able to work on my own without any guidance. I'm brilliant at devising new approaches to make people do what I want them to.
I Well, you seem to have plenty of strengths, Jane. But what about your weaknesses?
J I like to make things happen. I get frustrated if too long is spent sitting around discussing issues without action. I used to feel anxious about giving presentations to lots of people, but I've worked hard at it, and I've been on a couple of courses which have made a huge difference.
I You certainly present yourself very well today, Jane. Why are you leaving your current job?
J Well, as I mentioned earlier, I'm just mad about animals. Working at Selfridges is very glamorous, but my heart isn't in it. I know I'm good at sales, and I want a job that combines my selling skills and love of animals. Think how good I'll be at selling something I'm passionate about!
I Where do you see yourself in five years' time?
J I would hope to be Perfect Petfood's most successful sales manager, inspiring a team of people to make this company an even greater success.
I Thanks! Do you have any questions for me?

UNIT 7

Exercise 9, parts 1 and 2

Not getting on

A = Anya S = Sophie

A What's wrong, Sophie?
S Oh, nothing much, Anya.
A What do you mean? You look absolutely terrible!
S Oh, I'm just a bit upset, that's all.
A What about? It's not Charlie again, is it?
S Well, yes. He made one or two hurtful remarks this evening.
A One or two? He's always criticizing you these days! I don't know how you can stand it!
S Well, he's been having a bit of trouble at work recently, so he's quite stressed.
A Quite stressed? That's no excuse for being rude to his girlfriend, I don't think. I think his behaviour is totally out of order.
S Yeah, it's getting me down a bit, I must say.
A Well, you really mustn't put up with it any longer, Sophie. You should tell him that if he can't be nicer to you, you won't go out with him anymore.
S Oh, I suppose so. But the trouble is, I'm really crazy about him, you know.
A Well, that's obvious, or you wouldn't put up with all his terrible behaviour.
S And he loves me, too. I know it.
A Well, he's got a funny way of showing it, I must say.
S I suppose you're right. Our relationship hasn't been great lately. We haven't been getting on very well.
A You're not kidding. You've both been completely miserable. Honestly, Sophie, you must do something about it. It's no good waiting until things get magically better. It isn't going to happen.
S OK, OK, Anya! I'll talk to him tonight, I promise.
A Good! Now, put a smile on your face, and let's go and dance!
S All right, all right, just let me go and wash my face first. Can't go on the dance floor looking like this!
A Well, that's true. You could look a bit better than you do!
S Charming, I must say.
A That's more like it! You sound loads better already. Come on, let's go!

UNIT 9

Exercise 11, parts 1 and 2

A small disagreement

M = Megan H = Harry

M What are you watching?
H Shh!
M It's Saturday night and I can't believe you're watching a bunch of untalented singers all trying desperately to be a famous pop star.
H Shh! Sit down and be quiet! I can't hear the judges' comments.
M Well, if you want my opinion, it's contrived, over the top, and utterly predictable.
H You've changed your tune! When we were at university, this used to be your favourite show. We'd always watch it before we went out on a Saturday night, beers in hand, and giggling over the performances.
M Well, it was compulsive viewing then – it was a new type of reality show. The problem now is that it's the same cheesy format, the same tear-jerking stories to get the audience to feel sorry for them so they'll pick up the phone and vote. The whole thing's a joke!
H Well, I don't agree that it's a joke. There are lots of really talented singers on the show. What about that girl, Ella? She has a fabulous voice. And don't forget that boy band who won last year! They've had two number one hits!
M OK, OK, occasionally there's someone with a good voice. The point I'm trying to make is that most of them can't sing! That boy band only had those big hits because millions of teenage girls think they look cute. If you ask me, you're better off watching a good film rather than being manipulated by TV producers.
H To tell you the truth, I don't mind being manipulated. I'm not stupid. I know what you say is true, but I don't care. There's something enjoyable and addictive about the whole programme. The main point is not to take it too seriously, which you obviously do.
M What worries me is that you just haven't grown up yet. You still think of yourself as a student. I'm going to watch a film in the other room.
H Oh come on, Megan, just chill! Why don't you sit here on the sofa with me, and let's give the contestants a score out of ten, like we did in the old days at uni. I'll make some popcorn, too. It'll be fun.
M Oh, OK then! I suppose it was fun. Go on then! Move over!

UNIT 11

Exercise 10, parts 1, 2 and 3

Homeless to Harvard

C = Clare H = Harry

C I can't believe you're playing on the PlayStation when you have exams next month. I wish something would make you realize how important it is to work hard! I always wish I'd worked harder at school. I wasted so many years just watching TV!

H There you go! And you did OK.

C Eventually! But it took a long time to get my English degree, and I had to study when you and your brother were little. It would have been much easier if I'd just worked harder when I was your age.

H Mum, you're so predictable. You always say the same things. Give me a break!

C You just don't realize how lucky you are. I was reading on the Internet about this girl called Liz Murray; she went from sleeping on the streets to graduating from Harvard.

H Blimey! That's incredible! That is some journey. See, there's hope for me then! What happened to her?

C She grew up in one of the roughest parts of New York, and both her parents were drug addicts. And you think I'm bad because I nag you too much! She now speaks alongside people like Bill Clinton. I bet she would never have believed it when she was eating toothpaste with her sister because they were so hungry.

H Toothpaste! That is desperate. I can't imagine being so hungry that I'd want to eat toothpaste. They were poor. But mum, give it a rest, I'm only 15.

C Well, she was only 15 when her mum died, and then her dad couldn't pay the rent, so she had to sleep on the subway. But she never forgot her mother's mantra, 'one day life is going to get better', and she realized that if she didn't do something now, her life would never get better.

H Hmm! It didn't get better for her mum! So, what did she do? I mean, she was only 15 – she must have been pretty scared sleeping on the subway.

C She took herself to night classes to complete her high school education and did a year's work in a term whilst sleeping rough. Imagine that, Harry!

H Hmm! That is tough. It's hard enough to do school work anyway, let alone when you're homeless. So, how did she get her lucky break?

C Her teacher saw how determined she was and took her to visit Harvard. She decided there and then that she was going to go there. Through sheer hard work, she managed to get a scholarship from *The New York Times*, and now she's a successful author and speaker.

H Yeah, she does make me look a bit pathetic. Hey, but I did get 79% in my Maths test last week.

C Yes. So just think what you could achieve if you put your mind to it. Come on, Harry! When you're a grown man, you will never wish you'd spent more time playing on the PlayStation, but you might regret wasting so much time playing on it.

H OK, Mum! You've made your point. I'll go do some homework. There, PlayStation off, books open. Happy?

C Delirious! Remember, I don't nag you for my benefit. You'll kick yourself one day if you don't work hard now.

UNIT 12

Exercise 8, parts 1 and 2

You're never too old

N = Narrator M = Mary

N Mary Hobson is in her 80s, and nowhere near retirement. She gained a degree in Russian in her 60s, and a PhD at 74. She started learning ancient Greek at 77.

M I am what you might call a 'late developer'. I was 40 before I wrote my first novel, 62 when I went to university. My husband, Neil, was a talented jazz musician, but at 25 he developed a cerebral abscess, losing his speech, and the use of the right side of his body. We were so broke, we lived on national assistance for ages and did everything that was free.

I wrote my first novel while Neil had his weekly music therapy. That 50-minute session was all I had. I used to sit in the ABC cafe in Earls Court and write. Neil was terribly difficult. None of it was his fault, of course, but after 28 years, I thought: 'It's not my fault, either.' I left.

Having snatched a bit of life back, I had to do something with it. My daughter Emma gave me *War and Peace*, and I loved it so much. Then it hit me: I hadn't read it at all, I'd only read a translation, and I so longed to read the actual words. A marvellous, elderly Russian lady taught me the basics, and I enrolled on the Russian-language degree course at the University of London. People talk about 'the time of their lives'. Well, that was mine. Don't let anyone tell you your memory goes with age. Oh, the joy of learning!

I write poetry on buses and trains. I love London. Give me the town over the country any day. I try to go to Moscow every year in the coldest weather. My Russian friends think I'm mad; it hits minus 40, and they find it hellish. I adore lying in bed listening to snow being scraped from the pavements.

I have an overpowering feeling that I don't want to waste any time. I'm sure it's to do with atheism and acceptance of death. I am a dedicated atheist. I regard religion as complete lunacy. You've got one opportunity to be alive: for goodness' sake, don't waste it waiting for an afterlife. There's so much out there.

I won't be able to get out and about forever, so when I can't stagger down my front steps, I'll perfect my Greek. As long as I have my books, I'll be happy.

Answer key

Unit 1

1 1
2 'm … walking
3 've been walking
4 was taken
5 'll take
6 had taken
7 've had
8 were having
9 'll be having
10 are … made
11 has been made
12 'll have made
13 're being washed
14 had been washed
15 had been washing
16 sells
17 will be sold
19 'll have been teaching
20 were being taught

2

Active	Simple	Continuous
Present	sells	am walking
Past	walked	were having
Future	will take	will be having
Present Perfect	have had	have been walking
Past Perfect	had taken	had been washing
Future Perfect	will have made	will have been teaching
Passive	**Simple**	**Continuous**
Present	are made	are being washed
Past	was taken	were being taught
Future	will be sold	
Present Perfect	has been made	
Past Perfect	had been washed	
Future Perfect	will have been sold	

2
2 It's **been** really cold …
3 Manchester United **are playing** really well …
4 I've heard **you have passed** all your exams. Congratulations!
5 … when my friend **called**.
6 When I was a little girl, **I always spent** my pocket money on sweets.
7 **I've been going out** with Paulo for two years …
8 … Perhaps **I'll get** him a new shirt.
9 A one-day strike has **been** called by …
10 … Megan had been working hard and **deserved** to pass all her exams.

3
1 'm looking
2 don't understand
3 've … learned
4 'll call
5 've been doing
6 haven't seen
7 emailed
8 is studying
9 'll be accepted
10 has been chosen
11 's getting
12 'll shout
13 went
14 stayed
15 're saving
16 hadn't realized/didn't realize
17 have … been doing/were … doing
18 didn't hear
19 will be
20 'll look forward

4 1
1 Our house was built in the 17th century.
2 My flat's being decorated at the moment.
3 Has the coffee machine been fixed yet?
4 While the new kitchen was being built, we ate in restaurants.
5 When we went up to our hotel room, we found that it hadn't been cleaned.
6 She won't be recognized in those dark glasses.

2
1 were caught, left/were leaving
2 is … emptied
3 have been granted
4 were driving, were overtaken
5 had been snowing
6 arrive, 'll be picked up

5 1
1 moved
2 have been living/have lived
3 thought
4 'll miss
5 has been relocated
6 didn't want
7 'll have been
8 has lived
9 had … thought
10 joined
11 made
12 've been learning
13 don't like
14 get
15 's getting
16 'll be able to
17 misses
18 don't live
19 'll be
20 'll … miss

2
1 How long has he lived/been living in Japan?
2 Where did he move from?
3 Why did he move there/to Japan?
4 What did he do when he first arrived?
5 What has he been studying for three years?
6 Why doesn't he like writing Japanese?
7 What does he miss most?
8 When will he go back to Denver?

6
3 has (A)
4 have (F)
5 have (A)
6 didn't (A)
7 done (F)
8 does (A)
9 was (A)
10 is (A)
11 doing (F)
12 did (F)

7 1 **A** have … got/do … have
B 'm having
B Have … got/Do … have
2 **A** Have … got/Do … have
B haven't/don't, Have/Do
A 've had, 've got/have
B to have
3 **A** 've got/have
B haven't got/don't have
A had, Have
B 've got/have
4 **A** having, 've had, haven't had
B haven't got/don't have

8
1 blood
2 book
3 water
4 green
5 night
6 case
7 bag
8 rain
9 sun
10 road
11 air
12 day
13 hand
14 ice
15 land
16 card
17 sports
18 book

9 1 1 a 2 b 3 a 4 b 5 b 6 a

2
1 brought home to me
2 got on like a house on fire
3 make yourselves at home
4 brought the house down
5 as safe as houses
6 on the house

10 1
1 out
2 away/off
3 down
4 off
5 down/in
6 off, on
7 out
8 back
9 in
10 away/out

2
1 put … up (I), Put up (L)
2 sorted out (L), sort … out (I)
3 stand up (L), stand up (I)
4 take … off (L), take off (I)
5 picked … up (I), pick up (L)
6 Hold on (I), hold on (L)

11 1 ✓ dad's chicken curry, ✓ friends from home, ✓ living in a house

2 1 ✗ 2 ✗ 3 ✗ 4 ✓ 5 ✗ 6 ✗ 7 ✓

3 (I've) Just finished my first assignment
(Do you) Fancy tea and cake in my room to celebrate?
(I've) Always got time for cake.
(I) Know what you mean.
(It) Tastes yummy.
(I) Thought it was just me.
(I) Can't really do that here as our rooms are so small.
Students aren't the tidiest (people in the world).
(Do you) Want some more?

12 1
1 friend
2 English
3 clean
4 month
5 took
6 news
7 fans
8 box
9 thought
10 work
11 chart
12 winter

2

/e/	/ɪ/	/iː/	/ʌ/
letter	busy	freak	culprit
shelter	decide	sweeper	couple
dead	business	lethal	rough
/ʊ/	**/uː/**	**/æ/**	**/ɒ/**
woman	zoom	barrier	drop
should	drew	family	autobiography
goodness	suitable	accident	shock
/ɔː/	**/ɜː/**	**/ɑː/**	**/ə/**
water	birth	alarm	suspicious
abroad	earth	far	adopt
orphanage	Sir	father	beggar

Unit 2

1
1 He's written three magazine articles so far.
He's been writing a travel blog since he left home.
2 They've missed the bus again.
They've been missing you lots, so come home soon.
3 Paula's been leaving work early all this week.
Paula's left work early to run some errands.
4 I've lost my car keys.
I've been losing weight recently.
5 She's been talking on the phone for ages.
She's talked about this subject before.
6 The cat's been going next door to have its dinner.
The cat's gone upstairs.
7 He's had a heart attack.
He's been having second thoughts about the job.
8 I've been saving up to buy a brand new 52-inch TV.
I've saved up about £500.
9 I've been swimming, which is why my hair is wet.
I've swum 20 lengths today.
10 I've been finding it hard to concentrate recently.
I've found my cheque book at last.

2
1 have climbed
2 scaled
3 have been dumping
4 melts
5 are turning
6 have been working
7 are now being shown
8 was collected
9 includes
10 was looking
11 had
12 range
13 will be going
14 are trying

3
1 the 1700s
2 were … known
3 did, walk the tightrope
4 happened, all fell off the tightrope and survived
5 have, been known as, Since
6 How old was, fell
7 was, born, in 1979

4 1
1 becomes
2 has been trying
3 has been granted
4 holds
5 started
6 have been spraying
7 has been blasted
8 We're playing
9 will be traversing
10 will be suspended
11 feels
12 didn't want
13 are broadcasting
14 being shown

2
2 has been performing, performed
3 'm having, 've had
4 are you thinking, think
5 was banging, 've … banged
6 've been reading, read
7 fought, Have you been fighting
8 'm expecting, expect
9 is being decorated, is decorated
10 be losing, has lost

5 1 2 Have the street lights been repaired yet?
3 Some new anti-drug laws have just been passed.
4 No new homes have been built for 20 years.
5 The plants haven't been watered.

2 2 Bankers' bonuses have been slashed.
3 Fishermen have been rescued dramatically in the Pacific Ocean.
4 Over 400 people have been killed in the monsoon in Pakistan.
5 A Dali painting has been stolen in New York.
6 Ancient pyramids have been discovered in Sudan.
7 A missing teenager has been found alive.
8 Four hundred and sixty-four jobs have been axed in a shock announcement by the Council.

6 1 2 have her ears pierced
3 have my eyes tested
4 have had their car serviced
5 had our television repaired yet

2 Recently …
She's had the wedding dress made.
They've had the cake decorated.
Yesterday …
They had the champagne delivered.
He had his hair cut.
Today …
She's having her hair styled.
They're having the flowers delivered.
Next week …
They'll have had the photos developed.
They'll have had her wedding dress and his suit dry-cleaned.

7 1 a tour operator
b Ecuadorian Amazon
c travel writer
d Vienna
e film director
f the Navajo Nation

2 1 VS 2 GB 3 KM 4 KM 5 GB 6 VS

3 1 ✓ 2 ✗ 3 ✗ 4 ✓ 5 ✗ 6 ✗

4 **stunning** views/destination/places/hotel
friendly atmosphere/welcome/places/hotel/
romantic fire/views/haunt/destination/places/hotel/atmosphere
enchanting views/haunt/destination/places/hotel/atmosphere
adventurous tourist
sunlit terrace
crackling fire
interesting destination/places/hotel/alternatives
enthusiastic welcome
five-star hotel
perfect views/haunt/destination/hotel/atmosphere

8 1

	car	bus	bike	train	plane	ship/ferry
get into/out of	✓					
get on/off		✓	✓	✓	✓	✓
take off					✓	
land					✓	
ride			✓			
drive	✓	✓		✓		
catch		✓		✓	✓	✓
miss		✓		✓	✓	✓
board		✓		✓	✓	✓
park	✓	✓				

2 **car:** traffic lights, one-way street, Customs, traffic warden, horn, seat belt, service station, tyres, traffic jam
bus: traffic lights, one-way street, horn, season ticket, timetable, deck, ticket inspector, tyres, traffic jam
bike: helmet, traffic lights, one-way street, tyres, cycle lane
train: season ticket, track, baggage rack, Customs, platform, trolley, horn, timetable, aisle/window seat, ticket inspector, carriage
plane: runway, Customs, security check, life jacket, trolley, check-in desk, timetable, aisle/window seat, tyres, hand luggage, overhead locker
ship/ferry: Customs, cabin, harbour, life jacket, trolley, horn, timetable, deck, port

9 1 at
2 out of
3 across/into/to
4 to
5 through
6 towards
7 off
8 onto
9 over
10 into
11 past/through
12 to
13 into
14 against/on
15 in
16 out of
17 along
18 past
19 across
20 over
21 up/along
22 onto

10 1 1 explorer, exploration
2 politics, politician
3 photograph, photographer
4 luxury, luxurious
5 produce, production
6 Japan, Japanese

2, 3

●⬤	●⬤●	⬤●●
produce Japan success reject pollute complain	explorer production instructor authentic illegal	politics photograph luxury paradise scientists backpacker infinite Philippines packaging charity
●●⬤	**●●⬤●**	**●⬤●●**
Japanese afternoon Bangladesh	exploration politician disappointment destination European	photographer luxurious adrenaline spectacular memorial community Cambodia emergency

Unit 3

1 2 saved
3 had been
4 came through
5 was drowning
6 had arrived
7 had been bodyboarding
8 swept
9 had seen
10 swam
11 had managed
12 was struggling
13 hovered
14 was lowered
15 was airlifted
16 made
17 were

2 1, 2 1 stuck ✓
2 had stuck ✓
3 fell ✗
4 had fallen ✗
5 cost ✓
6 had cost ✓
7 had never flown ✗
8 flew ✗
9 had caught ✓
10 caught ✓
11 were ✗
12 had been ✗

3 1 was living, met
2 played, were winning, lost
3 wasn't thinking, had
4 was coughing, didn't get
5 was snowing, got up, were making, put, raced
6 was playing, hit, made
7 happened, was walking, noticed, wanted, vanished
8 was sunbathing, heard, appeared, landed

4 1 2 a 3 c 4 b 5 o 6 h 7 e 8 f 9 i 10 g 11 l 12 m 13 n 14 k 15 j

2 1 Two years ago, while I was working in Paris, my grandfather died.
2 As soon as I got home, I switched on the TV.
3 First I had a shower and then I got dressed.
4 Since I was a child, I had always wanted to visit Australia, and I finally went last year.
5 As he posted the letter, he realized that he hadn't put a stamp on it.
6 By the time he'd finished speaking, most of the audience had fallen asleep.
7 Once I'd told him the truth, I felt better.
8 Until I found a flat, I had stayed/been staying with friends for months.

5 2 A Roman temple was discovered underneath the new housing estate.
3 The races were held indoors because it was raining.
4 The swimming pool had been booked for a children's party on Saturday afternoon.
5 The dishwasher was being repaired, so I couldn't leave the house.
6 Our hotel room still hadn't been cleaned when we returned.
7 The fish hadn't been cooked for long enough.
8 New traffic lights were being put up at the crossroads.

6 1 saw
2 was … shown/released
3 were adored
4 has released
5 combines
6 are taken
7 worked
8 are studying
9 loathe
10 tells
11 overcome
12 become
13 directed
14 composed
15 has … made
16 has achieved
17 has come
18 will find

7 plot **T**, **B**; storyline **B**; chapter **B**; stalls **T**; critic **F**, **T**, **B**; director **F**, **T**; backstage **T**; trailer **F**; script **F**, **T**; rehearsal **T**; review **F**, **T**, **B**; e-reader **B**; character **F**, **T**, **B**; musical **F**, **T**; starring role **F**, **T**; novelist **B**; matinee **T**; prequel/sequel **F**; documentary **F**; blockbuster **F**, **B**; animation **F**; screen **F**; interval **T**; fairy tale **F**; programme **T**; whodunnit **B**; science fiction **F**, **B**; hardback **B**; dressing-room **T**; performance **F**, **T**; thriller **F**, **B**; playwright **T**; autobiography **B**; full house **T**; paperback **B**

8 1 2 i 3 b 4 g 5 j 6 h 7 a 8 f 9 e 10 c

2 1 turns up
2 setting off
3 Cheer up
4 stay in
5 settled down
6 broke up
7 find out
8 Shut up
9 Speak up
10 Hold on

9 1 1 had a relaxing afternoon
2 an article she's read
3 Alec Baldwin
4 his ex-wife
5 the same
6 an acrimonious
7 dating

2 1 b 2 c 3 e 4 a 5 f 6 d

10 1 1 pay /peɪ/ pear /peə/
2 write /raɪt/ wrote /rəʊt/
3 phone /fəʊn/ fine /faɪn/
4 round /raʊnd/ rained /reɪnd/
5 dear /dɪə/ dare /deə/
6 boy /bɔɪ/ beau /bəʊ/
7 tour /tʊə/ tow /təʊ/
8 fair /feə/ fear /fɪə/

2 3 /əʊ/ 4 /uː/
5 /ɔː/ 6 /ɜː/
7 /ɪə/ 8 /ɜː/
9 /ɔː/ 10 /ɜː/
11 /aʊ/ 12 /əʊ/
13 /uː/ 14 /əʊ/
15 /əʊz/ 16 /əʊs/ 17 /uːz/
18 /uːs/ 19 /uːz/
20 /əʊm/ 21 /uːm/ 22 /ɒm/
23 /ɒl/ 24 /əʊl/
25 /əʊm/ 26 /ʌm/
27 /eɪ/ 28 /eɪ/
29 /eɪ/ 30 /e/
31 /ʌ/ 32 /uː/ 33 /ʊ/
34 /əʊld/ 35 /ʊd/
36 /ʌ/ 37 /ɒ/ 38 /əʊ/

Unit 4

1 2 How long
3 Who made/directed the film 'Catch Me If You Can'?
4 How old was Frank when his parents
5 What was his first major con?
6 Which … did he
7 Where did he impersonate
8 Why did he (decide to) change course?
9 What did he teach (when he was a university professor)?
10 Where was he arrested?
11 Who starred as/played Frank in the movie/film ('Catch Me If You Can')?
12 Who does Frank work for now?/ Where does Frank work now?

2 1 2 how he learned to forge cheques
3 why his parents divorced
4 who decided to make a musical
5 which countries he visited
6 how he had the nerve to impersonate a doctor
7 why the police took so long to catch him
8 how he got the job with the FBI

2 1 how much money he made
2 what the film is called/what the title of the film is/what the name of the film is
3 which airline he flew for
4 who starred in the film ('Catch Me If You Can')
5 is working/works for the FBI?

3 1 2 by
3 to
4 at
5 on
6 in
7 about
8 of
9 with
10 from

2 2 What for?
3 Where to?
4 What about?
5 How long for?
6 Who for?
7 Who to?
8 What with?

4 1 don't
2 didn't
3 haven't

4 aren't
5 isn't
6 won't
7 'm not
8 doesn't
9 hadn't
10 hasn't
11 wasn't
12 weren't

5 1 a 2 b 3 c 4 d 5 f 6 e 7 g 8 h 9 j 10 i

6
1 not
2 no
3 None
4 not
5 not
6 n't
7 not
8 not
9 no
10 Not
11 none
12 no
13 n't
14 not
15 Not
16 none
17 no
18 no
19 None
20 Not

7
2 I don't suppose you've got change for a 20-euro note.
3 This machine doesn't seem to be working.
4 I didn't think it was going to rain.
5 They don't want their daughter to move to Canada.
6 I didn't expect to see you here.
7 I don't suppose you've seen Robert recently.
8 I don't think I'd like snails.
9 I don't expect you remember me.
10 I don't believe she passed all her exams.

8 1 1 E 2 C 3 H 4 A 5 D 6 G 7 F 8 B

2 2 C 3 A 4 E 5 D 6 B 7 F 8 G

9
2 for
3 of/from
4 from
5 in
6 to
7 in
8 in
9 to/with
10 to, about
11 at
12 in, with
13 for
14 in

10 1, 2

Adjectives	
untruthful	dishonest
incredible	unbelievable
implausible	ridiculous
improbable	unlikely
displeased	annoyed
abnormal	bizarre
unprofessional	amateur
unimportant	trivial
Nouns	
dishonesty	deceit
unreality	fantasy
disbelief	incredulity
Verbs	
disappear	vanish
misunderstand	confuse
mistrust/distrust	suspect
uncover	reveal

11 1
2 aren't you (fall)
3 wasn't it (fall)
4 could you (rise)
5 isn't he (fall)
6 isn't it (fall)
7 did he (rise)
8 have you (rise)
9 weren't we (fall)
10 would you (rise)

2
2 That was a really tasteless meal, wasn't it? (fall)
3 You've borrowed my new coat again, haven't you? (fall)
4 You couldn't/wouldn't water my plants, could/would you? (rise)
5 Vanessa, you're going on a business trip to Rome, aren't you? (rise)

Unit 5

1
1 You're going to work harder from now on, aren't you?
2 I'll see you next week, won't I?
3 Kate's leaving soon, isn't she?
4 You'll ring when you get there, won't you?
5 Our plane takes off at 4 p.m., doesn't it?
6 The painters will have finished by next week, won't they?
7 You aren't getting married next week, are you?
8 We won't need tickets to get in, will we?
9 We'll be millionaires one day, won't we?
10 Max won't be coming, will he?

2
1 'm going to, 'll
2 are going to, 'll
3 'm going to, 'll, 'll
4 will/is going to, 'll
5 's going to, 'll
6 'll/'m going to, 'm going to, 'll
7 'm going to, 'll
8 'll, 'll

3
2 I'll buy her a present.
3 I'm going to study hard for my exams.
4 I'm seeing/going to see the dentist next Friday.
5 I think Manchester United will win on Saturday.
6 I'm going to be late for the meeting.
7 My sister is expecting/having a baby in March.
8 My plane leaves at 7.30 a.m. (from London, Heathrow).
9 This time next week I'll be lying on a beach in Spain.
10 I think it'll be hot there.

4 1 work in the US (**J**); live in the north of England (**M**); move to London (**T**); travel the world (**T**); study law (**J**); buy a farm (**M**); win an Olympic medal (**M**); mix with celebrities (**J**); design swimwear (**M**); marry a film star (**J**); live near the river (**T**); buy a penthouse flat (**T**); go clubbing and partying (**J**)

2 *Sample answers:*
By the time Tommy is 30, …
3 he'll have bought a penthouse flat.
4 he'll be living near the River Thames.
5 he'll have travelled all over the world.

By the time Jack is 30, …
1 he'll have become a lawyer (for one of the best firms) in New York.
2 he'll be mixing with celebrities.
3 he'll have married a (rich) film star.
4 he'll be going clubbing and partying.

By the time Millie is 30, …
1 she'll be living in the north of England/the Lake District.
2 she'll have won an Olympic medal.
3 she'll have bought a farm.
4 she'll have designed her own brand of swimwear.

5
1 'm taking
2 'm going to be
3 'll be hoping
4 'll never give up
5 win
6 'll have been training
7 are being staged
8 'll have concentrated
9 will be

10 be hoping
11 will
12 will be

6 1 eat, won't get
2 won't move, 've found
3 'll love, meet
4 Will/Are … going to … learn, 're
5 won't go, have/have had
6 'll be, finish/'ve finished
7 don't do, will … have to
8 are, will deal
9 'll feel, 've had
10 've tried, 'll never use

7 2 **A** What are you doing/going to do
B ✓
3 **A** ✓
B What am I going to do?
4 **A** is going to the States
B ✓
5 **A** ✓
B You'll have to wake me up.
6 **A** ✓
B You'll be getting
7 **A** ✓
B It'll only take
8 **A** ✓
B We're going to stay at home.
9 **A** as soon as I arrive
B ✓
10 **A** ✓
B unless I get held up

8 1 taking
2 puts
3 putting
4 took
5 took
6 take
7 take
8 put
9 put
10 taken
11 put
12 take

9 1 a 're waiting for
b is expected
c looking forward to
2 a spend/'ve been spending/'ve spent/'m spending
b pass
c wasted
3 a Have … seen
b watched/were watching
c Look at
4 a Actually
b at the moment
c really
5 a owe
b borrowed
c lend

6 a embarrassed
b nervous
c angry

10 3 I couldn't take them all in.
4 I'll sort it out tomorrow.
5 Put it in your diary.
6 Please put them away.
7 … you'd better look after him.
8 I'll look into it right away.
9 Take it back!
10 … you've put me off her.

11 1 1 won't /əʊ/
2 walk /ɔː/
3 wonder /ʌ/
4 woman /ʊ/
5 warm /ɔː/
6 word /ɜː/
7 wear /eə/
8 weight /eɪ/
9 want /ɒ/
10 work /ɜː/
11 wander /ɒ/
12 women /ɪ/
13 worm /ɜː/
14 ward /ɔː/
15 weary /ɪə/
16 weird /ɪə/

2 1 phone /əʊ/
2 blood /ʌ/
3 love /ʌ/
4 through /uː/
5 weak /iː/
6 lower /əʊ/
7 north /ɔː/
8 height /aɪ/
9 pear /eə/
10 hear /ɪə/

Unit 6

1 1 cash
2 unemployment
3 traffic
4 luggage
5 food
6 music
7 violence
8 opportunity
9 ingredient
10 fluid

2 1 some, any
2 Some, any
3 some, any
4 any, any
5 some, some
6 any

3 2 Is there much work to be done in the garden?
3 I didn't spend much time on the homework.
4 Did they do much research before they found a cure?
5 I didn't have too many problems with this exercise either.
6 I've got too much luggage. I can't carry it all.
7 There is too much traffic on the streets of our town.
8 They couldn't give me much information about the delay to our flight.

4 1 *Sample answers:*
1 There are lots of cheese sandwiches.
2 There are a few chocolate biscuits.
3 There's a little vegetable curry and rice.
4 There isn't much rice or fruit salad.
5 There's a huge amount of spaghetti.
6 There are several hamburgers.
7 There are no chips or chocolate cake.
8 There aren't many tuna sandwiches.
9 There are a couple of doughnuts.
10 There's hardly any apple juice.

2 3 lots
4 a few
5 not much/hardly any
6 n't any/none
7 a little
8 a few
9 a little
10 some/a few
11 a couple of, lots/a huge amount

5 2 a few, a little
3 have less … than
4 few/very few
5 a little
6 Fewer
7 Few
8 a few
9 is … little
10 a few

6 1 1 somewhere
2 anyone/anybody
3 anywhere
4 anything
5 everything
6 nothing
7 Nobody/No one
8 nowhere
9 someone/somebody
10 something, anything
11 anyone/anybody
12 Everyone/Everybody

2 1 b 2 a 3 c 4 d 5 f 6 e
7 h 8 g 9 i 10 j 11 l 12 k
13 m 14 n 15 o 16 p

7 1 many
2 a bit
3 few

4 any
5 one of
6 all
7 one piece
8 all
9 a couple
10 nobody
11 anything
12 more
13 hundred
14 something
15 No one
16 a great deal
17 None
18 any
19 several
20 more than
21 everything

8 1 1 reduce
2 transfer
3 reclaim
4 compare
5 haggle
6 spread
7 set up
8 pay off

2 1 bargain
2 customer
3 the lowest
4 compare
5 hefty
6 charges
7 illegal
8 set up
9 leaves
10 slash
11 hike
12 outgoings

9 A **in** debt
under arrest
in Arabic
below/over/under 75%
below freezing
over/under 18 years old
on/against the advice
under new management
on holiday
under pressure
on business

B **during/in** the night
at/in/from the beginning
by/on New Year's Day
by/during/ in the winter
by/on Friday afternoon
at/by the weekend
in/on time
in a fortnight's time
during/in the rush hour
in his forties
at/by the end of the week

10 1 in
2 From
3 of
4 in
5 in
6 under
7 in/during
8 in
9 against
10 By
11 in
12 at
13 on
14 with
15 in
16 by
17 to
18 on
19 on
20 in

11 1 Sales representative (for a pet food company)

2 1 less than
2 much
3 one of the few
4 several
5 a great deal
6 some more
7 without any
8 lots of
9 a couple of

12 1 1 V 2 N 3 V 4 N 5 N 6 V 7 N 8 V 9 N 10 V 11 V 12 N

3 1 increase
2 present
3 invalid
4 protested
5 produce
6 present
7 minute
8 insult
9 content
10 contract

Unit 7

1 1 b 2 b 3 a 4 a 5 a 6 a 7 b 8 b

2 1 1 should/ought to/must/have to
2 Can/Could/May
3 must/have to
4 can/will
5 will/may/might/could
6 can/could
7 have to
8 must/should/ought to/may/might/could
9 can/could/ought to/must/should
10 have to/must/should

2 1 won't
2 don't have to
3 couldn't
4 won't
5 can't
6 was able to
7 mustn't

3 1 You mustn't/can't stop here.
2 We don't have to/needn't learn the whole poem.
3 They didn't have to take off their shoes.
4 He can't be speaking Swedish.
5 They won't have to wear a uniform at their new school.
6 You won't have to/need to help me do this exercise.

4 2 She must be missing her boyfriend.
3 It'll be Tom.
4 She can't still be sleeping.
5 They could be having a party.
6 He must have a deadline to meet.
7 It might be difficult to drive to work.
8 She may be hiding in the garden.

5 1 1 F 2 M 3 F 4 F 5 M 6 F 7 F 8 M

2 1 needn't/don't have to
2 mustn't
3 needn't/don't have to
4 need to/have to
5 don't need to/don't have to
6 got to
7 needs

6 1 ought to/should go
2 'll/might feel
3 have to/must finish
4 'll pass
5 should be touching down
6 must be
7 can't be
8 'll/could/might be snowing
9 can snow
10 must be making
11 could/might be
12 could/might be
13 don't have to hand
14 might/could go

7 1 1 can
2 have to/must
3 should/ought to/have to/must
4 can't
5 you must
6 can
7 have to/must
8 will
9 you should/ought to
10 I must/have to/need to
11 can always
12 can't
13 won't

14 you can
15 will
16 mustn't
17 could/can
18 You should
19 can

2 2 Guests are advised not to leave …
3 Using phones in the quiet carriage is not permitted.
4 He's bound to do well …
5 People under 18 are not supposed to drink alcohol.
6 The use of dictionaries in this exam is not allowed.
7 Travellers to the States are required to have a visa./A visa is required for travellers to the States.
8 You are likely to find …/It is likely that you will find …
9 My parents didn't let me stay out …

8 2 off with
3 down on
4 on with
5 up for
6 away with
7 out of
8 out with
9 up with
10 on with, out with

9 1 1 c 2 b 3 b 4 c 5 a 6 b

2, 3 1 absolutely terrible (E)
2 a bit upset (U)
3 one or two hurtful (U)
4 a bit of trouble (U)
5 totally out of order (E)
6 down a bit (U)
7 really crazy about (E)
8 loads better (E)

10 1 doesn't
2 shouldn't
3 mustn't
4 promised
5 Australia
6 planks
7 adolescent
8 arranged
9 relationship
10 angry
11 excitement
12 impressed

11 2 **Rob** I think Frank earns more than me.
Stuart Well, I know he earns a lot more than me.
3 **Rob** He's thinking of buying a second-hand Mercedes.
Stuart What do you mean? He's already bought a brand new one.
4 **Rob** He's just bought two pairs of designer jeans.
Stuart Didn't you know that all Frank's clothes are designer labels?
5 **Rob** Does Frank have many stocks and shares?
Stuart He has loads of them.
6 **Rob** Isn't Frank in New York on business?
Stuart No, in fact he's in Florida on holiday.
7 **Rob** His latest girlfriend has long, blonde hair.
Stuart Really? The girl I saw him with had short, brown hair.

Unit 8

1 1 b 2 b 3 a 4 b 5 c 6 a 7 a 8 c

2 1 1 D 2 D 3 ND 4 D 5 ND 6 D 7 ND 8 D 9 ND 10 ND

2 1 I'd love to meet someone who could teach me how to cook.
2 We're looking for a house which/that has four bedrooms.
3 We went to see Romeo and Juliet, which I really enjoyed.
4 Do you know a shop which/that sells second-hand furniture?
5 Marilyn Monroe, whose real name was Norma Jean Baker, died of a drug overdose.
6 I find people who lose their temper easily difficult to get on with.
7 My computer, which I bought only last year, is already out of date.
8 I met a girl you went to school with.
9 Professor Brian Cox, who is a well-known physicist and TV presenter, will give a talk next week.
10 I bought a cheese and pickle sandwich, which I ate immediately.

3 4 The thing I most regret is not going to university.
5 My two daughters, who are 16 and 13, are both interested in dancing.
6 no change
7 no change
8 The phone I bought yesterday doesn't work.
9 no change
10 The Algarve, where my mother's family comes from, is famous for its beautiful beaches and dramatic coastline.
11 no change
12 Salt, whose qualities have been known since prehistoric times, is used to season and preserve food.

4 1 2 what I believe to be right.
3 which was a nightmare.
4 where my brother lives.
5 whose body was covered in tattoos.
6 which came as a bit of a surprise.
7 when you expect to arrive.
8 whatever you want.

2 1 who 2 that/which 3 where 4 which 5 — 6 whose 7 which 8 — 9 — 10 that 11 whose 12 — 13 where 14 which 15 Whatever

5 2 She's a friend (who) I can always rely on.
3 That's the man (who) the police were looking for.
4 She recommended a book by Robert Palmer, who I'd never heard of.
5 The trainers (that) you paid £200 for have been reduced to £100.
6 This is the book (that) I was telling you about.
7 The Prime Minister, whose views I agree with, gave a good speech.
8 He spoke about the environment, which I care deeply about.
9 What's that music you're listening to?
10 My mother, who I looked after for many years, died last week.

6 3 screaming
4 satisfied
5 disgusting
6 confusing
7 challenging
8 conceited
9 frightening
10 exhausting
11 disappointing
12 tiring
13 unexpected
14 disturbing
15 thrilling
16 amusing
17 disappointed
18 well-behaved
19 promising
20 loaded

7 1 2 People living in blocks of flats …
3 Letters posted before …
4 The train standing on …
5 Firemen have rescued passengers trapped …
6 … house overlooking the River Thames.
7 … litter dropped by the crowds.

2 2 passing
3 stolen
4 saying
5 Feeling
6 borrowed
7 explaining
8 Taking
9 studying

8 1 known as Fearless Felix
2 who jumped
3 whose skydiving career
4 that scared him
5 whose fear of being enclosed
6 Terrified of wearing
7 knowing he had to
8 from which he would leap
9 which can happen when
10 including his mother and his girlfriend
11 what no man has done
12 which has put him

9 1 **People:** loyal, humble, stubborn, conceited, arrogant, considerate
Places: unspoilt, overcrowded, picturesque, breathtaking, desolate, built-up
Things: waterproof, smashed, automatic, cracked, priceless, handmade

2 1 breathtaking 2 arrogant
3 automatic 4 considerate
5 unspoilt 6 picturesque
7 stubborn 8 handmade
9 overcrowded

10 1 a ten-pound note
2 an eight-week language course
3 a six-hour drive
4 a three-course meal
5 a one-month holiday
6 a four-hour delay
7 a 100-page document
8 a three-year university course
9 a ten-year prison sentence
10 a five-star hotel
11 a 30-mph-speed limit
12 a 200-year-old house

11 1 of 2 with, for 3 for 4 of
5 of 6 in/with 7 to, to 8 about
9 to 10 of 11 of 12 for 13 for
14 with 15 about

12 1 **Silent consonants:** fasten, exhausted, whistle, straight, fascinating, delighted, debt, honest

No silent consonants: executive, inhabitant, distinctly, rebuilt, eccentric, insect, lamp, sumptuous, anonymous, citizen, documentary, landscape, temperature, business

2 1 sign 2 psychiatrist 3 handsome
4 island 5 Christmas 6 frightened
7 climber 8 grandfather
9 knowledge 10 calm

Unit 9

1 1 g 2 d 3 h 4 f 5 i 6 j 7 c
8 b 9 a 10 e

2 1 a He's always mending his motorbike in the living room.
b He will mend his motorbike in the living room.
2 a My brother is always leaving the top off the toothpaste.
b My brother will leave the top off the toothpaste.
3 a He won't help with the household chores.
4 a My sister is always borrowing my clothes without asking (me).
b My sister will borrow my clothes without asking (me).
5 a My grandpa won't let anyone choose what's on TV.
6 a My grandma is always gossiping about the neighbours.
b My grandma will gossip about the neighbours.
7 a Carole and Alan are always boasting about their children.
b Carole and Alan will boast about their children.

3 1 used to 2 used to 3 Did you use to
4 didn't use to 5 Did you use to
6 didn't use to 7 did you use to
8 Did you use to

4 1 He's always watching sports programmes on TV.
2 She would give us extra lessons after school./She was always giving us homework.
3 Our cat would always sleep on *my* bed.
4 My boss is always asking me to stay late.
5 My children will never help out at home.

5 2 a, b, c 3 a 4 a, b, c 5 a, b, c
6 a 7 a, b, c 8 a, b 9 a
10 a, b, c 11 a, b 12 a, b, c

6 1 1 aren't used to 2 get used to
3 'm used to, get used to 4 got used to
5 used to 6 didn't use to 7 's used to
8 get used to 9 did … use to
10 Have … got used to

2 1 get upset
2 'm getting better
3 to be a pilot
4 'll be ready, 'm … getting dressed, 've been ready
5 're lost
6 have got engaged
7 get to know
8 gets dark

7 1 2 a 3 c 4 c 5 c 6 a 7 a 8 a
9 a 10 c 11 c 12 c 13 c 14 c
15 c 16 a 17 a 18 b 19 a
20 c 21 c 22 c 23 a 24 b
25 a 26 b 27 c 28 a 29 b

2 1 used 2 would 3 used 4 wasn't
5 got 6 got 7 used, would
8 used, got

8 2 wave 3 point 4 right 5 suit
6 fair 7 fan 8 band

9 1 a bored
b board
2 a allowed
b aloud
3 a caught
b court
4 a loan
b lone
5 a hire
b higher

10 1 1 f 2 i 3 l 4 b 5 h 6 g 7 c
8 e 9 d 10 a 11 j 12 k

2 1 broke into
2 looked up to
3 take … back
4 pointed … out
5 come up with
6 told … off
7 deal with
8 fit in with
9 drop out of
10 count on
11 brought … up
12 break off

11 1 1 ✗ They are arguing about a TV programme he is watching.
2 ✓
3 ✗ These programmes always used to make them laugh/giggle.
4 ✓
5 ✗ Last year's winner was a boy band.
6 ✗ Harry doesn't take these shows (too) seriously.
7 ✓
8 ✗ Harry persuades Megan to watch the TV programme with him.

2 1 contrived, utterly 2 cheesy
3 joke 4 can't sing 5 better
6 manipulated 7 don't care
8 seriously, obviously

12 1 2 Sue isn't going to learn from the experience, but Tom is.
3 I've heard that you're thinking of moving from London. Are you?
4 They have dinner at seven, don't they?
5 You'll be able to get a ticket for me, won't you?
6 I've got no idea who this letter's from.
7 Can't you remember who Bill used to work for?
8 I've been waiting for you to come. Where were you?

9 We 'd been looking forward to coming for ages, then at the last minute we weren't able to.
10 Won't you sit down for a couple of minutes?

2 A What are you doing at the weekend?
B I haven't decided yet.
A We're going to Scotland. Do you want to come, too?
B I'd love to. Where are you staying?
A We've decided to camp. None of us can afford to pay for a hotel.
B Camping in Scotland in October! You'll be freezing cold.
A No, we won't, we've got strong tents, lots of warm clothes, and thick sleeping bags.
B Have you checked the weather forecast?
A Of course we have, and it's pretty warm for October.
B OK then. It'll be quite an adventure!
A Excellent! I'll tell the others – they'll be delighted. We'll pick you up at six on Friday. See you then. Goodbye!
B Bye!

Unit 10

1
2 I had to take the pills three times a day.
3 They must have been away on holiday.
4 We couldn't have a lunch break – there was too much to do.
5 He can't have been a millionaire.
6 We weren't allowed to shout in the classroom.
7 He wouldn't go to bed.
8 That will have been John on the phone.
9 You should have been more careful.
10 You could have helped with the washing-up for a change.

2 1 3 ✓✓ 4 ✓ 5 ✓ 6 ✓✓ 7 ✓✓ 8 ✓✓ 9 ✓✓ 10 ✓ 11 ✓ 12 ✓

2 *Sample answers:*
If I go to Norway, I can/will/may/might see the fjords.
If I went to Norway, I might/would/could see the fjords.
If I'd gone to Norway, I might/would/could have seen the fjords.

3 1
1 She must have got engaged to Andy.
2 They must have been doing something naughty.
3 She must have been making a cake.
4 They might have gone without me.
5 He can't have had a party last night.
6 They must have arrived home by now.
7 She might/must have mislaid my number.
8 He can't have cut it for ages.

2
1 It must have been blown down by the wind.
2 They must have been washed with something red.
3 It can't have been repaired properly.
4 It can't have been dry-cleaned recently.
5 It must have been hit by a stone.

4
1 could have used
2 might have climbed up
3 needn't have bothered
4 must have been joking
5 can't have spent
6 might have misheard
7 should have phoned
8 may have been delayed
9 needn't have worried
10 wouldn't have burned/got burned
11 must have fallen
12 can't have put on

5
1 shouldn't have
2 may have, 'll have
3 'd have, could have, might have, 'd have, needn't have, should have
4 must have

6 1
2 should … have come back
3 must have been
4 must have seemed
5 could not have survived
6 would … have dragged
7 could have imagined
8 must have got
9 must have been involved
10 might have received
11 must have lied/been lying
12 could have put
13 might not have acted
14 should not have committed
15 should not have come back

2 1 ✗ 2 ✓ 3 ✗ 4 ✗ 5 ✓ 6 ✗ 7 ✗ 8 ✓

7
1 all fingers and thumbs
2 heart-to-heart
3 all ears
4 out of my mind
5 enter your head
6 cold feet
7 give me a hand
8 hands full
9 face the facts
10 put on a brave face

8 1

Physical appearance	Personality
graceful	moody
wrinkled	big-headed
bald	brainy
well-built	quick-thinking
smart	nosy
curly	cheeky
clean-shaven	narrow-minded
tanned	affectionate
	smart
	hard-hearted

2 1 handed 2 elbow 3 thumbed 4 eyed 5 foot 6 headed 7 are armed 8 shoulder

9
2 remind … of
3 congratulated … on
4 models … on
5 hide … from
6 held … to
7 invited … to
8 trick … into
9 inherit … from
10 shouted … at
11 forgive … for
12 was accused … of

10 1

should	good	food	nude
bread	said	leaf	chief
choose	lose	taught	court
toes	knows	chef	deaf
hate	weight	through	knew
tight	height	wore	pour
full	wool	brain	reign
pool	fool	leave	grieve
blood	mud	foot	put

2 **The Pelican**
A rare old bird is a pelican
His beak can hold more than his belly can
He can take in his beak
Enough food for a week
And I'm damned if I know how the hell he can!

The Lady from Twickenham
There was a young lady from Twickenham
Whose shoes were too tight to walk quick in them
She came back from a walk
Looking whiter than chalk
And she took them both off and was sick in them!

Unit 11

1 1 1, 4, 8 refer to real past time. The others are all hypotheses.

2 2, 5, 8 refer to real past time. The others are all hypotheses.

3 2 don't 3 didn't 4 can't 5 is
6 won't 7 does 8 was/have
9 don't/haven't

2 1 I wish you were rich.
I wish you could/would/had come.
I wish I were rich.
I wish I could/had come.

2 1 could/was able to 2 wasn't
3 had 4 hadn't gone 5 have stayed
6 didn't speak/wouldn't speak
7 'd fallen 8 lived

3 1 1 I wish I'd invited him to the party.
2 You should have been watching the road.
3 If only I hadn't said that to her.
4 I wish I hadn't hit him.
5 I'd rather you didn't tell her.
6 I wish Meg wouldn't stay out so late.
7 I should have told him (that) I loved him.

2 *Sample answers:*
1 I wish I had a Rolls Royce.
2 If only I could get a job/had somewhere to live.
3 If only I could get to sleep.
4 We should have booked some rooms.
5 I wish I'd bought some petrol.
6 Cat: 'I wish she'd stop playing!'

4 1 If
2 hadn't
3 should
4 would
5 'd
6 only
7 wouldn't
8 should
9 would
10 could
11 couldn't
12 could
13 If
14 realized
15 wouldn't
16 imagine
17 won't
18 unless
19 have

5 1 1 I wish I had been true to myself.
2 I wish I hadn't worked so hard!
3 I wish I had said what I was really thinking.
4 I wish we had stayed in touch.
5 I wish I had done more!

2 1 spent more time/played more (2)
2 had taken (5)
3 been too scared (3)
4 stayed in touch (4)
5 fulfilled (1)

3 1 I wouldn't have been ill if I hadn't had the shellfish.
2 I would have phoned you if I had had the time.
3 If I had known the jumper wasn't machine-washable, I wouldn't have bought it.
4 I wouldn't have believed it if I hadn't seen it with my own eyes.

4 2 If I'd known your address, I could/would have sent you a postcard.
3 If I'd remembered when your birthday was, I would have bought you a present.
4 If I hadn't been taking my wife to the hospital, I wouldn't have broken the speed limit.
5 If I hadn't forgotten to set my alarm clock, I wouldn't have been late.

6 1 feel, won't go
2 sold, 'd make
3 see, 'll tell
4 hadn't gone, wouldn't have met
5 didn't love, wouldn't marry/wouldn't be marrying/wouldn't have married
6 buy, get
7 would … do, saw, would run
8 had brought. wouldn't be
9 hadn't had, would have burned down
10 were, 'd apologize
11 eats/had eaten, gets/would have got
12 had listened, would have heard, wouldn't be

7 1 1 Imagine
2 in case
3 unless
4 Unless
5 Suppose
6 in case
7 Had
8 Should

2 1 I won't come unless they invite me.
2 Supposing he left you, what would you do?
3 Suppose you had learned to play tennis, would you have been a champion by now?
4 We're going to install a smoke alarm in case there's a fire.
5 She won't get that job unless she learns to speak French.
6 Imagine the lifeguard hadn't been there; what would have happened?
7 I won't go out this evening in case Justin rings.
8 I'll be at my desk until 6.00 should you need to speak to me about the matter.

8 1 illegible
2 unreadable
3 childish
4 childlike
5 sensitive
6 sensible
7 truthful
8 true
9 intolerant
10 intolerable
11 economic
12 economical

9 1 breakdown
2 comeback
3 check-up
4 outcome
5 outlook
6 outbreak
7 breakthrough
8 feedback
9 takeaway
10 downfall

10 1 1 d 2 a 3 b 4 c 5 e 6 h
7 g 8 i 9 j 10 f

2 1 c 2 a 3 b 4 d 5 f 6 e

3 1 C 2 H 3 C 4 C 5 H 6 C
7 H

11 2 /e/ **bread:** jealous, leapt, breath, thread, breadth, deaf, health, meant, death, lead (n), weapon
/iː/ **meat:** beast, heal, lead (v), breathe, reason, scream, cheat, leap
/ɪə/ **fear:** dear, hear, clear, tear (n), beard, theatre, weary, gear
/eə/ **wear:** swear, tear (v), bear, pear
/eɪ/ **break:** steak, great
/ɜː/ **learn:** pearl, earth, search

Unit 12

1 1 1 a 2 the 3 the 4 a 5 –, a, the
6 the 7 a, – 8 the, –
9 a, The, –, the

2 1 A 2 the 3 a 4 – 5 a 6 a
7 – 8 the 9 – 10 the 11 the
12 the 13 a 14 – 15 – 16 –
17 a 18 the 19 The 20 an
21 the 22 the 23 – 24 the

2 1 1 everything
2 Everything
3 All
4 Every
5 All
6 All
7 everything
8 all
9 Every
10 everybody

2 1 All, none
2 either, both
3 both, neither
4 every
5 no, every
6 every
7 Each
8 either, both
9 Neither
10 Either
11 both, either
12 Each

3 1 These 2 This 3 That 4 those 5 that 6 that 7 this 8 these 9 this 10 this 11 that 12 this 13 That 14 those 15 that

4 1 the
2 a couple of
3 his
4 a great deal of
5 This
6 several
7 enough
8 the
9 little
10 both
11 This
12 no
13 the
14 every
15 a
16 many of
17 more
18 nobody
19 anything
20 some
21 his
22 the
23 a wealth of
24 a
25 one
26 these
27 most
28 an
29 all
30 the

5 1 back of the chair
2 cat's milk
3 toilet paper
4 parents' advice
5 bottle of wine
6 road sign
7 wine bottles
8 Prime Minister's duties
9 heel of my shoe
10 hairbrush
11 end of the film
12 today's news
13 Underground station
14 parents' wedding anniversary
15 company's success/success of the company
16 fortnight's holiday
17 government's economic policy
18 rate of inflation
19 coffee cups
20 cup of coffee

6 1 **be:** on the safe side, in touch with sb, no point in doing sth, on one's mind, up to date
have: the nerve to do sth, a word with sb, no chance of doing sth

2 2 have the right to
3 will be in touch with
4 is … on my mind
5 have a word with
6 had the nerve to
7 to be on the safe side
8 have no chance of
9 is no point in
10 be up to date

7 1 out of
2 in
3 on, by
4 for
5 in
6 between
7 for
8 to
9 about/on
10 with
11 to
12 of
13 before/by
14 in
15 to

8 1 1 ✗ 2 ✓ 3 ✗ 4 ✓ 5 ✗ 6 ✗ 7 ✗ 8 ✓

2 1 you might call
2 so broke
3 None of it
4 hit me
5 Give me … over
6 get out and about
7 stagger down
8 As long as

3 2 Her husband was **a** talented jazz musician.
3 She believes that you've only got **one** life so you mustn't waste it.
4 Mary decided to learn ~~the~~ Russian and Greek.
5 She read ~~the~~ all of *War and Peace* in Russian.
6 She prefers the town over **the** countryside.
7 She loves lying in ~~the~~ bed listening to the snow.
8 He lost **his** speech and the use of the right side of his body.

9

Noun		Verb	
advice	/əd'vaɪs/	to advise	/əd'vaɪz/
use	/juːs/	to use	/juːz/
abuse	/ə'bjuːs/	to abuse	/ə'bjuːz/
belief	/bɪ'liːf/	to believe	/bɪ'liːv/
relief	/rɪ'liːf/	to relieve	/rɪ'liːv/
grief	/griːf/	to grieve	/griːv/
excuse	/ɪk'skjuːs/	to excuse	/ɪk'skjuːz/
breath	/breθ/	to breathe	/briːð/
half	/hɑːf/	to halve	/hɑːv/
house	/haʊs/	to house	/haʊz/
safe	/seɪf/	to save	/seɪv/
bath	/bɑːθ/	to bathe	/beɪð/

10 2 **B** I did it. Sorry.
3 **B** I knew Johann was coming.
4 **B** I knew that ages ago.
5 **B** I didn't tell her.
6 **B** I didn't tell her.
7 **B** I told you.
8 **B** I like Annie.
9 **B** I do like Annie. I think she's great.
10 **B** I like her.

Irregular verbs

Base form	Past Simple	Past participle	Base form	Past Simple	Past participle
be	was/were	been	leave	left	left
beat	beat	beaten	lend	lent	lent
become	became	become	let	let	let
begin	began	begun	lie	lay	lain
bend	bent	bent	light	lighted/lit	lighted/lit
bite	bit	bitten	lose	lost	lost
blow	blew	blown	make	made	made
break	broke	broken	mean	meant	meant
bring	brought	brought	meet	met	met
build	built	built	must	had to	had to
buy	bought	bought	pay	paid	paid
can	could	been able	put	put	put
catch	caught	caught	read /ri:d/	read /red/	read /red/
choose	chose	chosen	ride	rode	ridden
come	came	come	ring	rang	rung
cost	cost	cost	rise	rose	risen
cut	cut	cut	run	ran	run
dig	dug	dug	say	said	said
do	did	done	see	saw	seen
draw	drew	drawn	sell	sold	sold
dream	dreamed/dreamt	dreamed/dreamt	send	sent	sent
drink	drank	drunk	set	set	set
drive	drove	driven	shake	shook	shaken
eat	ate	eaten	shine	shone	shone
fall	fell	fallen	shoot	shot	shot
feed	fed	fed	show	showed	shown
feel	felt	felt	shut	shut	shut
fight	fought	fought	sing	sang	sung
find	found	found	sink	sank	sunk
fit	fit	fit	sit	sat	sat
fly	flew	flown	sleep	slept	slept
forget	forgot	forgotten	slide	slid	slid
forgive	forgave	forgiven	speak	spoke	spoken
freeze	froze	frozen	spend	spent	spent
get	got	got	spoil	spoiled/spoilt	spoiled/spoilt
give	gave	given	spread	spread	spread
go	went	been/gone	stand	stood	stood
grow	grew	grown	steal	stole	stolen
hang	hanged/hung	hanged/hung	stick	stuck	stuck
have	had	had	swim	swam	swum
hear	heard	heard	take	took	taken
hide	hid	hidden	teach	taught	taught
hit	hit	hit	tear	tore	torn
hold	held	held	tell	told	told
hurt	hurt	hurt	think	thought	thought
keep	kept	kept	throw	threw	thrown
kneel	knelt	knelt	understand	understood	understood
know	knew	known	wake	woke	woken
lay	laid	laid	wear	wore	worn
lead	led	led	win	won	won
learn	learned/learnt	learned/learnt	write	wrote	written

Phonetic symbols

Consonants

1	/p/	as in	**pen** /pen/
2	/b/	as in	**big** /bɪg/
3	/t/	as in	**tea** /ti:/
4	/d/	as in	**do** /du:/
5	/k/	as in	**cat** /kæt/
6	/g/	as in	**go** /gəʊ/
7	/f/	as in	**four** /fɔ:/
8	/v/	as in	**very** /'veri/
9	/s/	as in	**son** /sʌn/
10	/z/	as in	**zoo** /zu:/
11	/l/	as in	**live** /lɪv/
12	/m/	as in	**my** /maɪ/
13	/n/	as in	**near** /nɪə/
14	/h /	as in	**happy** /'hæpi/
15	/r/	as in	**red** /red/
16	/j/	as in	**yes** /jes/
17	/w/	as in	**want** /wɒnt/
18	/θ/	as in	**thanks** /θæŋks/
19	/ð/	as in	**the** /ðə/
20	/ʃ/	as in	**she** /ʃi:/
21	/ʒ/	as in	**television** /'telɪvɪʒn/
22	/tʃ/	as in	**child** /tʃaɪld/
23	/dʒ/	as in	**German** /'dʒɜ:mən/
24	/ŋ/	as in	**English** /'ɪŋglɪʃ/

Vowels

25	/i:/	as in	**see** /si:/
26	/ɪ/	as in	**his** /hɪz/
27	/i/	as in	**twenty** /'twenti/
28	/e/	as in	**ten** /ten/
29	/æ/	as in	**stamp** /stæmp/
30	/ɑ:/	as in	**father** /'fɑ:ðə/
31	/ɒ/	as in	**hot** /hɒt/
32	/ɔ:/	as in	**morning** /'mɔ:nɪŋ/
33	/ʊ/	as in	**football** /'fʊtbɔ:l/
34	/u:/	as in	**you** /ju:/
35	/ʌ/	as in	**sun** /sʌn/
36	/ɜ:/	as in	**learn** /lɜ:n/
37	/ə/	as in	**letter** /'letə/

Diphthongs (two vowels together)

38	/eɪ/	as in	**name** /neɪm /
39	/əʊ/	as in	**no** /nəʊ/
40	/aɪ /	as in	**my** /maɪ /
41	/aʊ/	as in	**how** /haʊ/
42	/ɔɪ/	as in	**boy** /bɔɪ/
43	/ɪə/	as in	**hear** /hɪə/
44	/eə/	as in	**where** /weə/
45	/ʊə/	as in	**tour** /tʊə/

Notes

Notes

Notes

UNIVERSITY PRESS

Great Clarendon Street, Oxford, OX2 6DP, United Kingdom

Oxford University Press is a department of the University of Oxford. It furthers the University's objective of excellence in research, scholarship, and education by publishing worldwide. Oxford is a registered trade mark of Oxford University Press in the UK and in certain other countries

First published in 2014
2020 2019
10 9 8 7 6 5

ISBN: 978 0 19 471883 7

Printed in China

This book is printed on paper from certified and well-managed sources

ACKNOWLEDGEMENTS

Illustrations by: Gill Button pp.8, 9, 14, 23, 29, 36, 39, 53, 61, 69; Ian Baker pp.19, 28, 30, 48, 59, 65; Martin Sanders pp.7 (map),18 (map); Simon Cooper pp.38, 57, 62, 71

We would also like to thank the following for permission to reproduce the following photographs: Alamy pp.5 (couple/Image Source), 5 (computer camera/Art Directors & TRIP), 6/7 (skyline/Steve Vidler), 16/17 (taxi/Alex Segre), 43 (oil rig/Eye Ubiquitous), 48 (hiding/Todd Bannor), 49 (ACE STOCK LIMITED), 55 (nobleIMAGES), 60 (Imagestate Media Partners Limited - Impact Photos), 67 (canoe/BRStockPhoto - The Great Outdoors), 71 (Marianne/i love images/ women's lifestyle), 72 (woman/Catchlight Visual Services), 81 (Ben Molyneux People); Ardea p.50 (Thomas Dressler); CartoonStock pp.27 (Joe Kohl), 74 (S Harris), 78 (Alex Matthews), 80 (Dave Carpenter); Corbis UK Ltd pp.11 (art/ Stringer/Nepal/Reuters), 12 (family/Bettmann), 15 (city/Julian Elliott/Robert Harding World Imagery), 15 (Eco-lodge/Alison Wright), 77 (Jdc/Lwa); Getty Images pp.6 (kids/Sean Murphy), 11 (rubbish/NAMGYAL SHERPA/AFP/Getty Images), 15 (horses/Education Images/UIG), 15 (Vicky/Michael Bodmann), 15 (Kay/Tuan Tran), 15 (Gary/Jason Todd), 22 (talking/Olivier Lantzendörffer), 34/35 (Rob Lewine), 42 (small brick/Vincenzo Lombardo), 42 (large brick/ Vincenzo Lombardo), 43 (shake hands/Erik Isakson), 47 (Joan Vicent Cantó Roig), 58 (Vincent Besnault), 63 (uniquely india), 64 (Sjoerd van der Wal), 71 (Sue/Tom Fullum), 73 (Judith Haeusler); LEGO Group p.42 (small logo); 42 (large logo), 42 (family); Magmatic Ltd p.40 (Trunki); Moones p.56; Oxford University Press pp.5 (woman/Fancy), 10 (Gareth Boden), 13 (Niagara/ Photodisc), 32 (Millie/KidStock), 32 (Jack/Image Source), 32 (Tommy/i love images), 41 (BananaStock), 71 (George/Moodboard); Pal Hansen p.82; Press Association Images pp.24 (LANDOV), 25 (singing/Associated Press); Rex Features pp.12/13 (Nic Wallenda/Canadian Press/Rex Features), 17 (arrivals board/Haydn West/Rex Features), 18 (Prince WIlliam/SAC Faye Storer/Rex Features), 21 (crowd/Walt Disney Pictures/courtesy Everett Collection/Rex Features), 21 (doorway/Walt Disney Pictures/courtesy Everett Collection/Rex Features), 22 (poster/Universal/Everett/Rex Features), 40 (SwimFin/KPA/Zuma/ Rex Features), 54 (astronaut/KeystoneUSA-ZUMA/Rex Features), 54 (spaceship/ KeystoneUSA-ZUMA/Rex Features), 67 (couple/Rex Features), 67 (mugshot/Rex Features), 79 (man/c.Sony Pics/Everett/Rex Features), 79 (poster/c.Sony Pics/ Everett/Rex Features); Ronald Grant Archive p.25 (poster); She Who Dares p.40 (Game); Shutterstock pp.5 (computer mac/Igor Klimov), 16 (Joe/Corepics VOF), 31 (Cartoonresource), 33 (Galina Barskaya), 37 (serg_dibrova), 43 (tax form/RTimages), 51 (Levent Konuk), 72 (sign/Andy Dean Photography)

The authors and publisher are grateful to those who have given permission to reproduce the following extracts and adaptations of copyright material: p.82 'A Life in the Day of Mary Hobson' by Caroline Scott, The Sunday Times Magazine, 30 November 2003. Reproduced by permission of NI Syndication.

Although every effort has been made to trace and contact copyright holders before publication, this has not been possible in some cases. We apologise for any apparent infringement of copyright and, if notified, the publisher will be pleased to rectify any errors or omissions at the earliest possible opportunity.